AF496495

WEMBLEY

STADIUM OF LEGENDS

First published in the United Kingdom in 2007 by

Dewi Lewis Media Ltd
8, Broomfield Road
Heaton Moor
Stockport SK4 4ND
England

www.dewilewismedia.com

ISBN: 9780954684396

Design & artwork production: Dewi Lewis Media
Print: 1010 Printing International

WEMBLEY

STADIUM OF LEGENDS

PETE TOMSETT & CHRIS BRAND

dewi lewis media ltd

This book is dedicated by Chris

to Susie, Holly and Timmy
'Love conquers all; let us also yield to love' – Virgil

…and by Pete to

Ruby M.A. (of Woolwich)
'You brought new light to my tired eyes,
You brought new love to my jaded heart'
(Greenwich Park, The Skywhales – 2005)

Contents

One of the majestic twin towers of the old Wembley

Foreword

"In a world that has developed so great a devotion to sport, there is no arena that can compare with Wembley's"

While this may sound like a line from publicity material for the new Wembley, it is a quote from the 1924 Official Guide to the British Empire Exhibition, tempting visitors to the original stadium. And with good reason – for this was the biggest and best in the world at the time. Today, throughout the world you'll find people who know about Wembley and for decades it has held pride of place amongst the world's top venues.

It's now taken as read that Wembley's main purpose is football, with the occasional rugby league and a few concerts. Yet the original Wembley wasn't built specifically with football in mind. That was simply how history played out, with football increasingly dominating as it grew in stature, particularly after 1966. In fact, sixteen different sports have taken place there at one time or another – American football, athletics, baseball, boxing, football, Gaelic football, greyhound racing, hockey, hurling, lacrosse, rugby league, rugby union, show jumping, speedway, stock-car racing and wrestling.

By the 1990s though, the place that Pele called '*The Church of Football*', had really begun to show its age. After a long and active life, our beloved stadium was in poor health. The piecemeal modernisation that had taken place over the years was just not going to be good enough anymore, and eventually the difficult decision was taken to build a new state of the art stadium with facilities worthy of a venue of this prominence. So as we entered the new millennium, Wembley began a major transformation and a magnificent new stadium has now risen up from the rubble of the old. With its spectacular arch, the new building is already a dramatic addition to the London skyline, and it can only be a matter of time before new legends are created.

When the decision was taken to rebuild Wembley I was working in an office that overlooked the old stadium. Like most fans, I understood the need for a new national stadium and, personally I felt that it should be at Wembley. But I also still found it hard to believe that this much loved monument and site of England's finest two footballing hours was to be knocked down. However, it was exciting to see the plans for what was to come in its place and to be so close that I could see the project unfolding in front of me.

With this world famous piece of English sporting and cultural history being demolished, it struck me that there was an important story to tell. Of course most people know about the White Horse Cup Final, the '66 World Cup and Live Aid but there is so much more to the Wembley story. There were even many twists and turns of fate that led to the stadium being built there in the first place on the site of an earlier tourist attraction. Even after it was built, its future could have come to an abrupt halt after just three or four years had it not for the foresight, imagination and enterprise of one man – Arthur Elvin. In the decades that followed, the stadium grew and grew in profile to occupy a special place in the consciousness of the nation, if not the whole world.

Many of us quite naturally had misgivings about the loss of the twin towers, and the building of the new Wembley inevitably suffered from delays and problems. But at the end of the day, the new stadium is a spectacular building and it's the perfect stage for the best sportsmen and women to display their skills. I hope you enjoy our telling of the stadium's history and our record of the remarkable transition from old to new, as Wembley once again takes its place as one of the world's leading sporting venues.

Pete Tomsett

A reminder of Sir Edward Watkin on a road sign in Wembley

Before delving into the incredible sporting history of Wembley, there's another wonderful story to tell. But for a little twist of fate, it could all have been very different and the original Wembley Stadium might never have been built. Today, instead of admiring the gleaming early 21st century stadium now occupying the site, we could easily have been welcoming hordes of tourists and their hard-earned cash to London's equivalent of the Eiffel Tower.

The suburban bustle of Wembley that we know and ...er, love today, was still sparsely populated farmland criss-crossed by country lanes until well into the second half of the 1800s. In fact Wembley's population was recorded as a mere 209 in 1851. Elsewhere, London suburbia had begun to grow and entrepreneurs were looking at the potential for further major housing developments.

To try to speed up the process of population growth around north-west London, in the 1880s the Metropolitan Railway Company opened an extension to its Baker Street to Willesden Green line, out to Wembley Park and Harrow. Whilst it now provided a new fast connection to and from central London, on its own this coming of the railway wasn't enough to trigger the desired effect. Something else was needed.

The chairman of the company, Sir Edward Watkin – a major figure in English railways and an M.P. – bought up 280 acres of land close to the railway in Wembley. This was to be the first step in an ambitious grand plan to entice people to use his railway and venture out to the distant region just beyond the capital. He now needed a major new attraction to encourage people to visit this part of the county of Middlesex.

Having been impressed by the Eiffel Tower when visiting Paris in 1889, he aimed to build something similar, but even bigger and more grandiose. This would be the centrepiece of what would be a whole park, full of attractions, which he planned to name The Pleasure Gardens.

After Gustave Eiffel himself turned down the opportunity, Watkin and his Metropolitan Tower Construction Company held a competition to design this ambitious new monument. From the numerous weird and wonderful entries received, a design was chosen that was not too unlike the Eiffel Tower. It was to be 1150 feet tall (165 feet higher than Eiffel's in Paris) with stages at 155 feet and half-way. It was to extravagantly incorporate restaurants, theatres, novelties and exhibitions, along with a small viewing area at the top. Sir Benjamin Baker (1840-1907) was chosen as the engineer for the project, having already proven his ability by designing the Forth Bridge in Scotland and the Aswan Dam in Egypt.

At first things went well. In 1892 the tower's foundations were laid by the team who had just finished the Blackpool Tower. Meanwhile the Pleasure Gardens were constructed, with pagodas, bandstands, a lake and sports grounds. The building of the first stage of the tower itself

Sir Edward Watkin

began in June 1893 but took longer than expected, not being completed until late in 1895, a year and a half after the Pleasure Gardens had been opened to the public. The story was beginning to turn sour, but worse was to come. The first stage of the tower itself tower was not opened to the public until 1896, but by this time 77 year old Watkin's health was failing, and he decided to retire from the railways.

As for his grand project, work was already well behind schedule and the foundations had started to shift. Unable to raise further funds, the construction company went into voluntary liquidation in 1899.

Sir Edward died in 1901 and his tower closed to the public the following year, after further safety concerns. This optimistic episode was brought to a sad close with the tower being demolished in 1907.

The public and the press, fickle as always, labelled the tower as 'Watkin's Folly'. Yet in many ways Watkin was a man of vision, though perhaps just too far ahead of his time. An indication of this is one of his other grand ideas, which was to build a rail link that would stretch from Manchester, through London, and over to the continent via a channel tunnel.

Today, not only does the Channel Tunnel exist but we take it completely for granted. Though work started on the project, it seems that Watkin was perhaps being too ambitious for what was technically possible at the time. Just two miles of his channel tunnel project were dug before it was abandoned.

All that now remains of Sir Edward William Watkin's Wembley legacy is an obscure and very short road that bears his surname, located on an industrial estate that now occupies part of the local area. There is, however, a memorial to him in St Wilfred's Church in his home town of Northenden, on the southern outskirts of Manchester.

Although primarily a business project, Watkin's Tower and the Pleasure Gardens were also a romantic vision and would have been a wonderful legacy if they had been completed and had survived to this day. Today, Prague's Petrin Hill with its own 1890's Eiffel Tower copy gives an idea of what might have been.

Unfortunately no trace of the tower or gardens remain, but the partly developed space that was left behind, along with the convenient and fast rail link to London, was to prove the perfect location for another major project - The British Empire Exhibition. And this was to incorporate a major multi-purpose sports facility, The Empire Stadium.

Above: Metropolitan Railways 1890s leaflet showing the Pleasure Gardens and how the tower was going to look (Brent Archive)

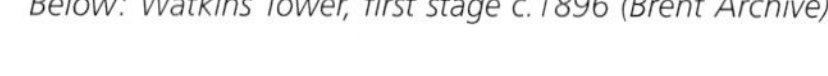

Below: Watkins Tower, first stage c.1896 (Brent Archive)

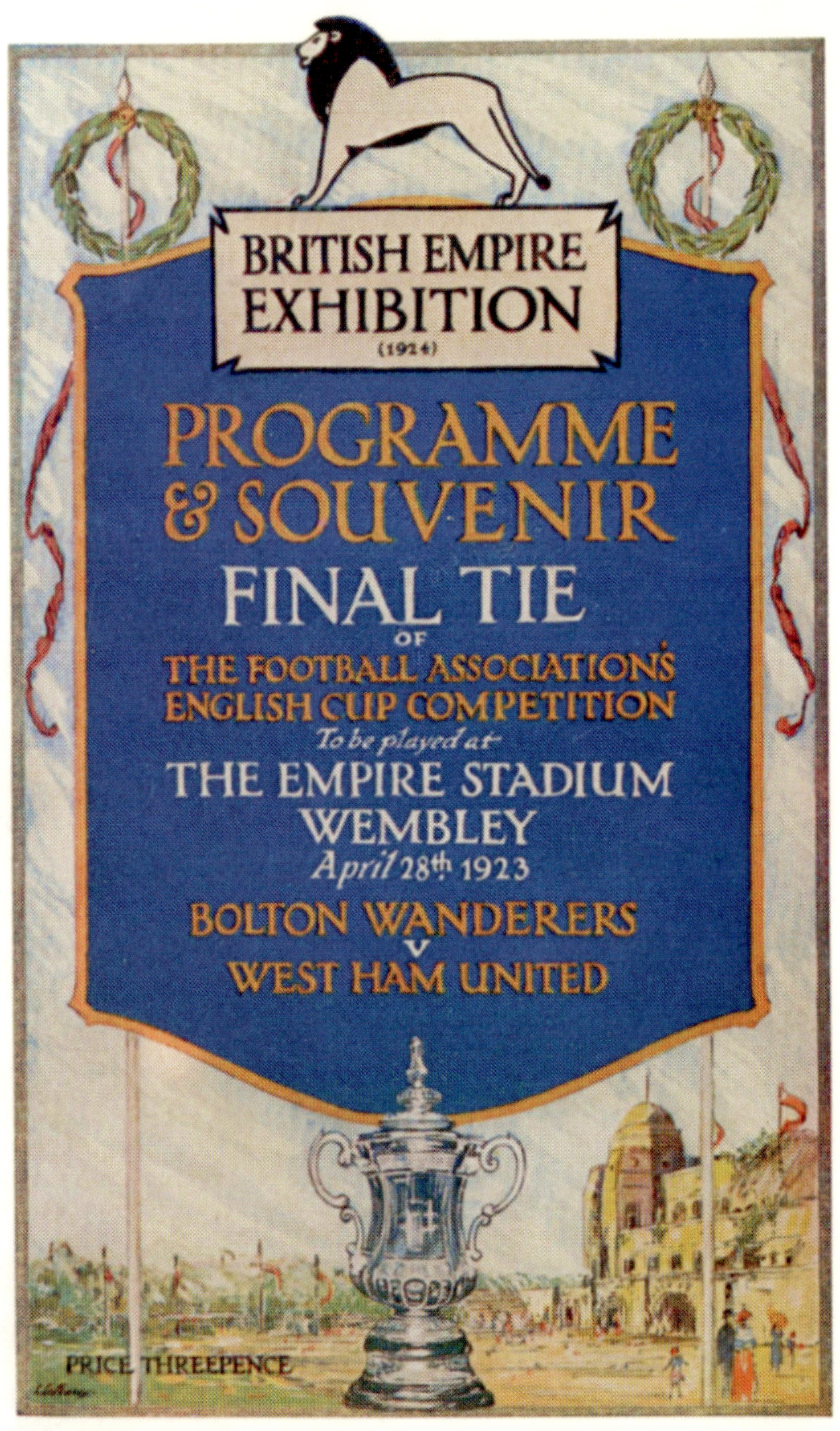

Programme from the first Wembley F.A. Cup Final in 1923 (Brent Archive)

Since the turn of the century there had been moves to hold a major exhibition in London to promote trade throughout the British Empire. After the 1914-18 World War the idea was revived and in 1920, with government backing, a company called The British Empire Exhibition Incorporated was set up to make it happen. They decided that the event would be held in 1924, and an area of 216 acres in Wembley was chosen for the location and purchased. This included the land on which Watkin's Tower had stood as well as the former Pleasure Gardens, which had been used as a Territorial Army training ground for a while before being turned into an eighteen hole golf course. Watkin's other legacy to north-west London was that of a fast rail connection from central London to Wembley Park station, very close to the site. This was an important factor in this decision, which was actually opposed by Wembley Urban District Council, who had earmarked the area for an up-market residential development.

The Football Association took a particular interest in the exhibition because the plans included a major multi-purpose sports stadium. Having decided many years before that their annual showpiece, the FA Cup Final, should always be held in London, they found themselves urgently needing a suitably prestigious venue. In the early years since its inception in 1872, the final had mostly been held at Kennington Oval, a cricket ground. From 1895 it was switched predominantly to Crystal Palace. However, during World War One this had been turned into an army depot and though it was due to become available again soon, there was no proper seating or stands, only grassed banking. For the first three finals after World War One Stamford Bridge had been used, though it was considered very unglamorous and unsuitable, and was essentially only being used by default. So the chance for the FA to use the biggest and grandest of new stadiums at Wembley was one that was too good to be missed. It would also be a better venue for some

of the English national team's home games. Since these commenced, also in 1872, they had been played at club grounds up and down the country. Internationals were still rare events for England though, and with the difficulty of overseas travel, games were only against other the other 'home' nations, Northern Ireland, Scotland and Wales.

Work on The Empire Stadium, as it was officially known, began on 10th January 1922 with the ceremonial first cutting of the turf by the Duke of York. Sir Robert McAlpine and Sons had been awarded the contract, with the bulk of their workforce being made up of ex-servicemen. In preparation for the stadium their first task was to remove the hundreds of thousands of tons of clay from the hill on which Watkin's Tower had stood. In the following months work commenced on the rest of the exhibition site, but the jewel in the crown, the stadium, was the priority.

Things were very different when the old Wembley came into being only a few short years after the end of World War One. It was a period of great change. Television was still many years away and the fledgling BBC (British Broadcasting Company as it was then named) was just putting out its first radio broadcasts. Although car ownership was beginning to grow, you were still as likely to see horse drawn carts on the roads as the latest 'Model T' Fords. It was the era in which young people began to feel much more liberated, shaking off some of the more rigid social etiquette of Victorian times. For the better off 'Bright Young Things' it was the age of The Charleston, Noel Coward, and when smoking for women first became fashionable. Conversely, it was also a time of great hardship for many. Instead of a 'land fit for heroes', many servicemen returning from the horrors of the war found unemployment and poverty.

1920s Wembley Park was part of the area that became known as Metroland. Although the term was originally a clever piece of marketing from the Metropolitan Railway Company to encourage

CUP
APRIL 28TH
3. p.m.
AK ZINKEISEN

FINAL
WEMBLEY
LONDON TRANSPORT

Above: Aerial view of police clearing the pitch for the 1923 FA Cup Final (Brent Archive)

Below: Empire Stadium and nearby Exhibition buildings 1924 (Brent Archive)

development of the area served by their railway, it soon became part of the language. There was a genuine pride and affection for this new suburbia, gently rising north-westwards from London and cutting a swathe across the county of Middlesex. Poet John Betjeman was amongst those who captured its essence, with the countryside and the new housing merging harmoniously along the Metropolitan railway line. He even compared it to a river meeting the sea:

'When melancholy autumn comes to Wembley
And electric trains are lighted after tea
The poplars near the stadium are trembly
With their tap and tap and whispering to me
Like the sound of little breakers
Spreading out along the surfline
When the estuary's filling, with the sea'

The national and international context of the day was also very different, still influenced by a Victorian legacy and trying to rebuild after the horrors of World War One. As the Empire Exhibition was to emphasise, Britain under the reign of King George V still possessed an empire stretching around the globe. A changing political climate led to the election of the first Labour government in late 1923, with Ramsay McDonald as Prime Minister. But this was to survive a mere ten months, with Stanley Baldwin's Conservatives regaining control in 1924.

At Wembley, construction of the stadium took a mere 300 working days, finishing in April 1923. The distinctive twin towers that were to become the building's trademark, echoing the exotic domes of palaces on the Indian sub-continent, were the design of architects Sir John Simpson and Maxwell Ayrton. As with most other buildings for the exhibition, the stadium was constructed using the relatively new material of ferro-concrete; 25,000 tons of it.

While it wasn't to everyone's taste, the stadium was a spectacular sight. As the Official Exhibition Guide later put it, *'There is not in all England a modern building that can compete with the Empire Stadium in the effect it creates upon the mind of the spectator'*. On completion, the stadium measured 900 by 650 feet, with the towers each 126 feet tall. Estimates of the overall cost vary from around £500,000 to £750,000. As well as the pitch for football and other sports and entertainment, a running track was constructed around the perimeter. Safety tests that were carried out included the odd spectacle of over a thousand men marching, sitting and standing in formation around the stands to ensure that they could cope with the movements of match-day crowds.

The new stadium's completion was timed to perfection. Just three weeks later on 28th April 1923 it was opened to the public for its first event. This was the 48th FA Cup Final in which First Division Bolton Wanderers played West Ham United, then top of the Second Division. The scorer of the first Bolton goal that day, and therefore the first-ever Wembley goal, was their inside right David Jack, who scored after only two minutes. Jack Smith got a second for Bolton early in the second half to give Wanderers a 2-0 victory.

Unfortunately for both Jacks, the game is better known as 'The White Horse Final' after one of the mounted police officers, PC George Scorey and his horse Billy, brought the excessive crowds under control and cleared the pitch, enabling the game to take place. The ground capacity was 127,000, which the FA had anticipated would be more than enough. But with tickets being available on the day with an admission price of one florin (ten pence), perhaps double that number tried to attend. It's believed that well over 200,000 somehow crammed in to see the match, including at least 75,000 who climbed the walls or rushed the gates to get in. As kick-off time approached, the situation looked impossible with the crowds entirely covering the pitch. Two marching bands, there to entertain the fans, were simply swamped but somehow managed to keep playing amidst the mayhem. King George V was in attendance and officials advised him to leave for safety reasons, but he declined to do so.

Perhaps it was the distinctiveness of Scorey's white horse, along with the good nature of the crowd, but somehow the playing area was cleared and kick-off was only 45 minutes late. Scorey himself credited his horse with seeming to know what was needed. What is certain is that were it not for the actions of PC Scorey and his colleagues, the match would have had to be postponed, potentially

Surviving buildings from the 1924 British Empire Exhibition

causing further chaos and ill-feeling. Even so, for the entire game the crowd were continually spilling on to the pitch, with the police having to clear space each time a corner was taken. Despite being sent tickets for subsequent year's cup finals, it's said that PC Scorey was simply not interested in football and never attended another game. The FA learnt their lesson that day and every Cup Final since has been all-ticket.

Before the British Empire Exhibition commenced, another football first was squeezed in. On the 12th April 1924 Wembley hosted its first football international, with England drawing 1-1 with Scotland before a surprisingly low crowd of 37,250. England fielded a very inexperienced line-up, averaging only four caps each, including Bolton striker David Jack, scorer of the first ever Wembley goal.

Despite the awe-inspiring new stadium, this was the start of an era of mixed form for the England team. The FA twice withdrawing from FIFA during this period didn't help, greatly reducing the range of potential opponents for the national side. In fact it would be four more years before there was even a second home international at Wembley.

The British Empire Exhibition, then the largest ever event held in Britain, was opened by George V on 23rd April 1924. When the King gave his opening speech it was the first time a monarch had broadcast on the radio. The Official Guide described the exhibition's purpose as *'to stimulate trade, to strengthen the bonds that bind the Mother country to her Sister States and Daughter Nations'*. The event covered 219 acres and attracted over 27 million visitors, 4.5 million to the stadium alone,

Few remnants of the other Empire Exhibitions buildings remain today. Those that do all look rather tarnished and their historical significance is neglected and forgotten. A couple more – a mock chapel and a façade, close to Wembley Arena – survived until 2005 but were pulled down to create space for the wider redevelopment.

including a further six month period in 1925 when it was re-opened. The site had a remarkable array of fountains, lakes and gardens, along with dozens of palaces and pavilions, each representing the architectural style of the countries exhibiting and showing off their goods and services; it was basically a huge shop window. This aspect was summed up in the exaggerated eloquence of the Official Guide: *'all the world of Wembley is in gala dress. The visitor sees here the ripe product of British achievement in all parts of the earth.'* Although one of the main aims of the exhibition was to educate people as to the diversity and breadth of the British colonies, it was widely felt that this point failed to penetrate the public consciousness. Most people left the exhibition having learned nothing about the colonies, but with fond memories of their funfair rides.

Although the exhibition was well served by stations at Wembley Park and Wembley Hill (now Wembley Stadium), the site was so vast that it had its own three-mile rail line, the Neverstop Railway. This was a loop line connecting Wembley Park with Exhibition Station and a stop close to the stadium. The carriages were moved by a revolving screw-thread running between the rails. If this wasn't enough there were also hundreds of bath chairs (wheeled bath-shaped chairs pushed by an attendant) available for hire at 2s 6d (12.5p). It's interesting to note that although the stadium was completed ahead of schedule, several other exhibition buildings failed to be finished in time for the formal opening due to industrial disputes. Some things never change! Amidst the exotic displays, The Empire Stadium itself presented a range of entertainments, such as performances by choirs and massed bands. Strangest of all, however, was a 'Great International Rodeo' featuring cowboys from far and wide.

While the coming of the Metropolitan Railway failed to attract enough people and development, the Exhibition and Stadium did finally succeed in putting Wembley on the map. Although the exhibition had been a popular and well-attended event, it was a financial failure making substantial losses. On 31st October 1925 its gates closed for the last time. The Government decided that the two-year run was long enough and the whole site was put up for

An old Wembley logo stencilled on a merchandise stall

sale. Initially, attempts were made to find buyers for individual buildings but this proved difficult as they had been designed as grand showcase structures and were not well-suited to other purposes. Eventually, in 1926, they were all sold to entrepreneur and speculator Jimmy White, though his ownership would prove to be short-lived.

With Wembley's future hanging in the balance, attention switched back to sport and in April 1927 the stadium witnessed the shock of Cardiff City beating Arsenal 1-0 and taking the *English* FA Cup out of England for the one and only time to date. Arsenal's Welsh goalkeeper, Dan Lewis, is said to have blamed his shiny, and therefore slippery, new jersey on letting a saveable shot slip under him for the Cardiff winner – that shot being from a Scotsman, Hugh Ferguson. With live radio broadcasts of football league games having begun three months earlier, the Cardiff-Arsenal game became the first Cup Final to be broadcast live. For Cardiff City it also made up for the disappointment of their first Wembley final two years previously, in which they had gone down by the only goal to Sheffield United. 1927 also saw the first singing of the hymn 'Abide With Me', which although it had no obvious connection with football, was to become a crowd favourite and a Cup Final tradition.

It was in the months following the 1927 Cup Final that the stadium's story could have come to an abrupt end after only four years. White had been selling off parts of the site and had brought in Arthur Elvin to carry out demolition work. Elvin had already worked at the site, having run tobacco kiosks during the exhibition but now rapidly found himself making a lot of money from the demolition, selling off a lot of the materials for scrap. In the meantime the stadium went into liquidation with White in serious financial trouble. In August that year, seizing his opportunity, Elvin raised the necessary money and bought it from White for £122,500. This was to turn out to be perhaps the most significant turning point in the stadium's history, setting it on its course to become the Wembley we now fondly reflect back on.

Although not yet thirty years old, Elvin had already led an eventful life, and the challenge of transforming Wembley's fortunes almost single-handed was something he was able to take in his stride. As a teenager in World War One he was an observer in the Royal Flying Corps and was shot down behind enemy lines. He was captured and, despite many attempts, failed to escape from German Prisoner of War camps. But escaping from the financial black clouds that hung over Wembley was another matter. His first important sporting innovation was to replace the running track surrounding the pitch with a dirt track and introduce greyhound racing. 1927 had seen an explosion in the sport's popularity throughout Britain and Elvin was keen to encourage it to his stadium. If he could establish regular and popular sporting events at Wembley it would generate enough income to pay for the stadium's day-to-day upkeep. The more prestigious events of football internationals and finals, whilst making money when they took place, simply weren't enough on their own to make the stadium economically viable, so Elvin exercised his good commercial brain and branched out into other sports.

The first greyhound meeting took place on 10th December 1927 and attracted a crowd of 50,000. There were some humorous teething problems though as in the third race the dogs actually caught up with the mechanical hare! A rumour that had circulated beforehand was that if this happened the dog touching the hare would be electrocuted, but this turned out to be untrue. Instead the race officials simply sped up the hare, which initially added to the comedy as it knocked over one of the dogs, but then the race was completed and the result allowed to stand. Wembley rapidly became popular with the punters, who would venture there from all over London and by 1928 the Wembley greyhound meetings were averaging a gate of 9,000. The first

step towards securing Wembley's financial survival had been successfully taken.

Step two was to attract another sport that cleverly made use of the cinder track the greyhounds already raced on; speedway. Known in its early days as 'dirt track', speedway was one of the few major sports not invented in Britain. It arrived in the 1920s from New South Wales, Australia but quickly gained popularity. By the 1930s it was often attracting larger crowds than many county cricket matches. From the outset close ties were established between the speedway and greyhound fraternities, due largely to their both being able to use the same facilities within stadiums. There was probably a sizeable overlap of spectators attending both the weekly greyhound and speedway meetings at the same grounds.

By 1929 speedway was averaging 6,000 strong crowds, though success had not been a foregone conclusion, but a calculated gamble by Elvin. It proved to be a winner, though some viewed the imported sport with a rather bizarre mixture of abhorrence and intrigue. In 1928, novelist and future Member of Parliament A.P Herbert wrote of Wembley's saviour, *'Heavens, the noise! It is like ten million mechanical drills performing in unison. It swells and falls as the riders take the corners; it echoes about the cavernous concrete halls, drowning the feeble acclamations of the crowd; it dies slowly as the riders stop, and the end of a race seems like the end of a battle. It is titanic and terrible and monstrous; and yet in that enormous place, made by those monsters, it seems appropriate and right. And I do believe I rather liked it.'*

The Wembley Lions speedway team was formed with Wembley Stadium as a home venue. The sport was to prove very popular and would be another regular source of income, putting the stadium on a much sounder footing. Thursday night was speedway night at Wembley, and the Lions were to race there for a total of 22 highly successful and memorable years. It's interesting to note that speedway and greyhound racing were the only two new sports launched in Britain in the 1920s and 1930s that sustained their popularity.

In the midst of these very positive changes, the English football team was taught a major lesson by

Façade of an Empire Exhibition building demolished in 2005

the visiting Scots, who inflicted the biggest margin of defeat at Wembley to this day. The Home International tie of 31st March 1928 was only the second international to take place at Wembley, some four years after it opened, and was played in heavy rain on an already sodden pitch. Playing skilful possession football and with a hat-trick from right winger Alec Jackson, the 'Wembley Wizards', as they became known, put a total of five goals past England goalkeeper Ted Hufton, regarded as the best goalkeeper in the world at the time. With a five-man forward line, and not one of them over five feet seven tall, the Scots – Jackson, Dunn, Gallacher, James and Morton ran riot. Outplayed for the bulk of the game, England belatedly managed a single consolation goal.

This was clearly a sound lesson for England, especially as the visiting team had been considered relatively weak beforehand. It all seemed to illustrate that the plucky amateurism of the English game was just not keeping pace with the world's developing football nations. The chopping and changing of the selection committee was certainly not helping with consistency and strategy. It was in fact an entirely different eleven from the England side that had played at Wembley in 1924 and there had even been ten different goalkeepers tried in that time. The fact that England's centre-forward that day was 21 year old Bill 'Dixie' Dean making his first Wembley appearance, and on the way to a record breaking 60 goals in a season, only emphasised that something was very wrong. Dean, on the other hand, could do little wrong in his early international appearances, in one spell scoring ten goals in five games, bagging a brace a game. He went on to score 17 goals for England in 16 matches and 473 goals in 502 matches in his career. This laudable achievement was even more remarkable considering he had earlier broken his skull in a motor-bike accident.

Looking to further diversify the stadium's activities and create more financial security, Elvin had by 1929 succeeded in bringing the Rugby League Challenge Cup Final to Wembley. The competition had started in 1897 and had taken place at various grounds in the sport's heartlands of the north of England, predominantly Yorkshire and Lancashire, but the governing body was attracted by the prestige that would come from holding their grand annual event in the capital. But it wasn't a straightforward journey to attract the north's showpiece final to the capital city's suburbs. At the 1928 annual Rugby League Conference, in Llandudno, the Chair of the Welsh Rugby League Commission John Leake suggested that the final be staged in London. After a narrow vote thirteen agreed, ten did not. Three London venues were suggested; Crystal Palace in the south of London, White City to the west and Wembley in the north. Arthur Elvin offered Wembley's facilities at a rate of 15% of the gate money. Being an astute businessman he included a clause that hiked it up to 25% for any subsequent years' usage. The deal was done.

> On the 31st October 1931 a record crowd for a greyhound meeting turned out to see that year's St Leger – the final race of Mick The Miller, considered the greatest racing greyhound of all time with 19 wins from 19 Wembley starts. Despite being five, old for a racing dog, he didn't disappoint his fans, scraping through to win by a nose from 'Virile Bill'. He was then led round for a lap of honour, his tail wagging happily, still undefeated in retirement. Wembley's Spring Cup in 1932 was won by Future Cutlet who in an extraordinary career was only unplaced on one occasion. The stadium's racing manager Captain Brice is said to have commented that he was the 'best looker of them all'.

And so it was, that, before a crowd of 41,500, Wigan of Lancashire confronted Dewsbury of Yorkshire in the first Wembley Rugby League Challenge Cup Final, on 4th May 1929. Ticket prices were set at between ten shillings and sixpence (52.5p) down to two shillings (10p) for the terraces. Whilst the fans filed in, the Welsh Guards played a selection of music to entertain them. A Mr Arthur Gaiger, in white coat, led the crowd singing 'Abide With Me', while amongst the spectators was a Mr W.H. Townsend, who had donned the Dewsbury team kit of cherry and white, and walked from the north down to Wembley. Would his stupendous effort be equalled on the field of play and produce the result he desired?

Wigan's Jim Sullivan was one of the greatest points scorers in the illustrious history of rugby league, kicking 2,687 points in a long career of 928 matches. It wasn't just on the rugby field that Jim performed well, as he also represented Wales at baseball and could even have become a professional golfer. Wigan were glad he stuck to rugby, even more so when as their captain, he became the first player to score in a Wembley Challenge Cup final. His penalty after three minutes set Wigan on their Wembley way. On fourteen minutes Wigan scored the first Wembley try, thanks to stand-off Syd Abram, the only Englishman to score in the final. This came after a 40 yard run into the corner. Dewsbury notched up their team's only points of the afternoon with Wembley's first drop goal, through Welsh full back Jack Davies. Wigan ensured victory with two tries, from the New Zealander, Lou Brown and the Scot, Roy Kinnear (father of comic actor Roy Kinnear). All-in-all it was a rather one-sided affair ending Wigan 13, Dewsbury 2.

Wembley's first rugby final was certainly an immediate financial success with gate receipts of £5,614 – some £2,000 higher than the previous Challenge Cup Final record set in 1924 at Rochdale. The final was thus set to become an annual pilgrimage south for the rugby league community. The only years that this wasn't the case were during World War Two with the finals understandably back in the north. Wembley also missed out on the Challenge Cup final in 1932, due to a football fixture already booked for that weekend. Instead that year's Final was held at Wigan.

Bolton Wanderers were amongst those who were delighted with the saving of Wembley, returning in April 1929 for their third Cup Final victory of the decade there, with a 2-0 win over Portsmouth. Five members of the Lancashire side that year played in all three of those victories (with David Jack scoring in both the 1923 and 1927 finals) perhaps emphasising the benefit of consistency and stability in a team, a lesson yet to be learnt by the national side.

The first FA Cup final of the 1930s was on April

A surviving building from the 1924 British Empire Exhibition

26th and enabled Arsenal to secure their first triumph in a final. Leading club manager of the time, Herbert Chapman had connections with both finalists, having enjoyed much success with their opponents for that day, Huddersfield Town, before leaving to manage Arsenal. The crowd paid £26,265 in gate receipts as Huddersfield succumbed to goals from Alex James and Jack Lambert. The final is remembered more so for the rather bizarre sight of the German airship Graf Zeppelin hovering ominously over the pitch during the match.

The 1930 Rugby League Challenge Cup Final between Widnes and St. Helens is still spoken off as one of the greatest Wembley shocks. The Widnes thirteen were all locals, with the exception of South African Van Rooven. St Helens had a team of stars but were no match for their Lancashire neighbours. Surprisingly all the points scored came in the first half and Widnes were jubilant at a 10-3 score line.

Two other football matches that Wembley staged in the year of 1930 were of lower profile. Clapton Orient of Division Three South encountered problems when they moved to a new ground at new Lea Bridge Speedway Stadium at the start of the 1930-31 season. The Football League ruled that the perimeter fences were too near the touchlines and ordered them to expand the pitch. Lea Bridge Speedway would not allow them to do so however, as it interfered with their racing track. Neighbouring football clubs Leyton FC and Walthamstow Avenue declined Clapton Orient's requests to play there, but a temporary solution was found in Wembley Stadium.

Arthur Elvin's eternal quest to generate income had included the possibility of leasing Wembley to a football league club. Orient's plight was an opportunity for just such an experiment. So it was that lowly Clapton Orient played two of their 'home' league fixtures across London in the cavernous Wembley Stadium. The first was against Brentford, just six miles from Wembley. This was a muddy encounter on 22nd November 1930, watched by a crowd of 10,300 and Orient eased to a 3-0 victory. A *Daily Herald* correspondent asked if Brentford would ever play at Wembley again. He also observed that the sacred turf had been a quagmire and might need relaying. The second match was against Southend United but a low turnout of

Aerial view of 1937 FA Cup Final (Brent Archive)

2,500 didn't cover the costs of staging the match. Orient's hosts at Lea Bridge agreed to alterations to their pitch, so they returned home, and the experiment was over. It had produced neither enough interest nor income for Wembley to stage league football on a regular basis.

The England football team played a number of internationals in the 1930s, but only seven were at Wembley, all against Scotland. They won the first three, in 1930, 1932 and 1933, drew in 1936 and lost in 1938. They were more successful in home matches at club grounds around the country, with a 6-2 win over Hungary at Highbury in 1936 and a 7-0 drubbing of Northern Ireland at Old Trafford in 1938.

After winning the London Cup against Crystal Palace in 1930, Wembley Lions established themselves in the top tier of speedway in the south of England in the 1931 season. They topped the Southern League with 59 points from their 38 matches, followed by Stamford Bridge and West Ham. Top riders for the team were Colin Watson and Jack Ormston. They also boasted the great Australian, Lionel Van Praag, who was to go onto to win the inaugural individual

world title later in the decade. The 1931 season also saw Wembley Lions take the National Cup and become the sport's first double winners. The first was against Brentford, themselves based just six miles from Wembley.

The FA Cup Final of 1933 saw another innovation. Lancashire rivals Everton and Manchester City had made the journey south to contest the final, and for the first time in a professional match players wore numbers on the backs of their shirts. But rather than the later practice of teams being numbered 1 to 11, it was decreed that Everton would wear numbers 1 to 11 and Manchester City 12 to 22. To further add to the confusion both teams, who usually wore blue, changed to avoid a colour clash. Appropriately enough Dixie Dean of Everton became the first player to wear the number nine. He scored as well to win his only Cup Final winner's medal. City goalkeeper Langford made mistakes which gifted Everton their first two goals as the whites of Everton beat the reds of Manchester City 3-0 with goals from Dunn, Dean and Stein.

The Challenge Cup Final of 1933 was also a notable match, with the Prince of Wales amongst the record crowd of 41,874 watching Huddersfield defeat Warrington 21-17 in a thrilling final. The Australian Kangaroos Rugby League side toured Britain twice in the 1930s, and as well as a series of matches in the north of England, played Wales at Wembley. In 1930 Australia won by 26 points to ten, and in 1933 Wales were on the end of an even heavier defeat; 51-19 to the Kangaroos.

The sport of baseball made two appearances in 1934, on the request of the American Ambassador to London. Two teams made up from the crew of the USS New Orleans faced each other. Later in the year American servicemen stationed in England also held a game, between the US Air Force and the US Ground Forces. So another sport was added to the what was becoming an impressive roll of honour for the stadium.

Meanwhile the event which literally set the ball rolling at Wembley, football, also hosted a memorable FA Cup Final that year, with Manchester City returning after the previous year's defeat to take on Portsmouth. Pompey took the lead after 26 minutes through Septimus Rutherford and held on until well into the second half. However, their centre-half Jimmy Allen was badly injured and had to be carried off midway through the second half. City took their opportunity with centre-forward Freddie Tilson striking twice, in the 73rd and 87th minutes to take the trophy for the Maine Road side. The tension of the closing moments proved too much for nineteen year old City goalkeeper, Frank Swift. Having been at fault over the Portsmouth goal, he was so emotional that he fainted after the final whistle.

The first Speedway World Championship Final was held at the Empire Stadium on 10th September 1936, with an estimated crowd of 93,000. It was so successful that Wembley became home for this crowning event of the speedway calendar for the next nineteen years. This event was for individuals rather than teams or countries, and the inaugural title went to an Australian, appropriately as they had invented the sport. Lionel Van Praag was the victorious rider. The following year the title went to the USA's Jack Milne, and the last competition before the war saw the title back in Australian hands, with Bluey Wilkinson winning in 1938.

The FA Cup Finals of 1937 and 1938 were very different from each other. In 1937 Sunderland were led by local lad Raich Carter and took on Preston North End. An exciting match produced four goals, Gurney, Carter and Burbank scoring for Sunderland and O'Donnell scoring the only Preston reply. Raich Carter may have captained his side to victory and scored into the bargain, but he blotted his copybook by dropping the famous trophy en route to the dressing room. Preston shook off the defeat and the next season another successful cup run took them back to Wembley. Unfortunately though, the 1938 FA Cup Final was an uninspired affair that looked like becoming the first Final to result in a draw since 1912. Huddersfield Town and Preston North End were goalless deep into extra-time. Then Huddersfield captain Alf Young tripped George Mutch on the edge of the penalty area. The referee awarded a penalty, which the dazed Mutch got up and took. The ball cannoned off the underside of the crossbar and in, which was enough to take the trophy to Deepdale. The goal was also the highlight of the match for the 10,000 television viewers watching the first cup final to be fully tele-

King George VI meets
Preston North End before
the 1937 FA Cup Final
(Brent Archive)

vised live. Still only in black and white, the broadcast signals only reached a privileged audience in south east England.

In rugby league, Salford reached the Challenge Cup Final in both 1938 and 1939, becoming the first team to play in Wembley finals two years running. The first of these resulted in a low scoring match against Barrow which they won by seven points to four. The two most enduring images from that day are not directly connected with rugby. Firstly the trophy was presented to Salford's Gus Risman by Australian cricketing legend Don Bradman. After the presentation Salford posed for what already had become the time-honoured triumphant team photo. It was a sign of the times that, whilst posing with the trophy, these healthy and successful young sportsmen were practically all smoking cigarettes. Their captain Gus Risman, a Welshman born of Latvian parents, was the only non-smoker and he had his hands full, parading the Challenge Cup atop his team-mates' shoulders. The following year, nicotine or not, Salford were not in such good health as they took on Halifax. With many of the Salfordians in the grip of flu, Halifax were the runaway winners by a 17 point margin as they trounced the holders 20-3. It was scant consolation for the Reds that another new attendance record of 55, 453 watched them suffer.

After its first decade, the experiment of rugby league Cup Finals in the rugby union and football dominated south certainly was paying off. Crowds were gradually increasing for the annual pilgrimage south, with extra interest being generated by some of the lesser known teams making it through to enjoy the glamour and prestige of the London event. Nearly 42,000 for the 1933 match, over 51,000 for Leeds' defeat of Warrington in 1938, and over 55,000 for the last final before World War Two, in 1939. And this at the time of some economic hardship, when ticket prices for many league matches in the north were being reduced for poverty-stricken supporters.

Late in April 1939, in what turned out to be the last FA Cup Final before World War Two, two teams with great footballing pedigree were on display – Wolverhampton Wanderers, who had just finished runners-up in the league to Everton, and Portsmouth who were at Wembley for the third time in ten years. Wolves were favourites with their young team built around centre-half and captain, Stan Cullis, but it was Portsmouth who went ahead after 29 minutes when a ball from Anderson found Bert Barlow who scored from twelve yards against his former club. Cries of 'Play up Pompey' were rewarded with a further goal two minutes before the interval, with Anderson notching up his seventh goal of a fine cup run. No sooner had the players finished their half time oranges and cups of tea, when Portsmouth grabbed a third. After a long shot from Barlow, the greasy ball was fumbled by Wolves custodian Scott, and Parker was on hand to shoot home the rebound. Dicky Dorsett pulled one back for the Wolves but Portsmouth went on to become only the second side to score four in a Wembley Cup Final when Parker headed in his second on 71 minutes. Nobody knew it at that time but as King George VI presented the trophy to Portsmouth captain Jimmy Guthrie, the FA Cup was about to begin a long stay in the hands of Pompey. War broke out that September, and the Cup was just one of many sporting competitions suspended for six earth-shattering years.

The outbreak of World War Two brought a suspension of sporting competition, with the Government at first prohibiting the gathering of large crowds. However, the powers that be soon realised just how vital competitive sport was going to be for the morale of the nation in such difficult times. Within weeks the decision was modified and adapted versions of football tournaments were cobbled together. Of Wembley's other regular sports, Rugby League held its finals in the north for the duration of the war, while speedway was suspended. Greyhound racing too was initially suspended, but brought back from Easter 1940.

Early on in the war Dr. Goebbels, Hitler's Minister of Propaganda, had boasted that because of the threat of the German air-force, the Luftwaffe, England would no longer be able to enjoy football on a Saturday afternoon until the Germans took control. But although life was very different, Wembley Stadium proudly never closed during the war. Fortunately it somehow managed to escape bomb damage, although a doodlebug (flying bomb) did hit and badly damage nearby kennels in August 1944. An unexpected additional wartime role came after Dunkirk, when the stadium was used as a temporary home for refugees and became an emergency dispersal centre.

Many players were in the armed forces, however, and had to request leave in order to take part in each match. Even the top stars of the day were not given any special treatment and had to make their own travel arrangements to get to even the biggest games. Despite there being no FA Cup Finals or Home International Championships during the war, Wembley still managed to host twenty-three matches – more than it would otherwise have done in peacetime! These mostly consisted of Football League War Cup matches and wartime internationals. The internationals involved representative sides of England, Scotland, Wales, Belgium and The Netherlands and attracted crowds of up to 90,000. Unfortunately from the players' perspective these were not considered as

official matches by the FA, and therefore no caps were awarded.

The first Football League War Cup Final took place in June 1940 at Wembley, between Blackburn Rovers and West Ham United, with the players all on a £1 win bonus. No-one was busier that day than Blackburn left half Frank Chivers. As well as playing football he was also a miner, and indeed was mining in Barnburgh Colliery near Doncaster until 4 a.m. on the day of the match. For safety reasons the police had limited the crowd to 50,000 but those not able to get a ticket listened to radio commentary by the BBC. There was a radio audience at home and at sea, with seamen tuning in to the 6 p.m. kick off on the ship's radio where they heard a goal from Sam Small win the cup for the Hammers. The following year's final – a 1-1 draw between Arsenal and Preston North End – was notable for being the first Wembley outing of an 18 year old Tom Finney for the Lancashire side, on his way to becoming probably the side's greatest ever player. Interestingly, although the rules allowed for extra-time, it couldn't be played due to the blackout – no outdoor lighting was permitted so that German bombers couldn't pick out landmarks from the air after dark.

The England v. Scotland encounter of January 1942 gave perhaps the biggest indication of how much fans would endure for the sake of still seeing organised sport. The match had almost been postponed after four days of heavy snow. However, the Prime Minister Winston Churchill and his wife were going to be special guests, so the Wembley staff pulled out all the stops to enable the game to go ahead. Arthur Elvin even got his ground staff to paint the lines on the frozen pitch in light-blue dye so they would be more clearly visible. Despite continuing heavy snowfall and freezing conditions, the match proceeded with the teams being presented to Mrs Churchill beforehand. On view for the Churchills and the 64,000 hardy fans who had made the trip were Tommy Lawton, Stanley Matthews and Dennis Compton for England, while

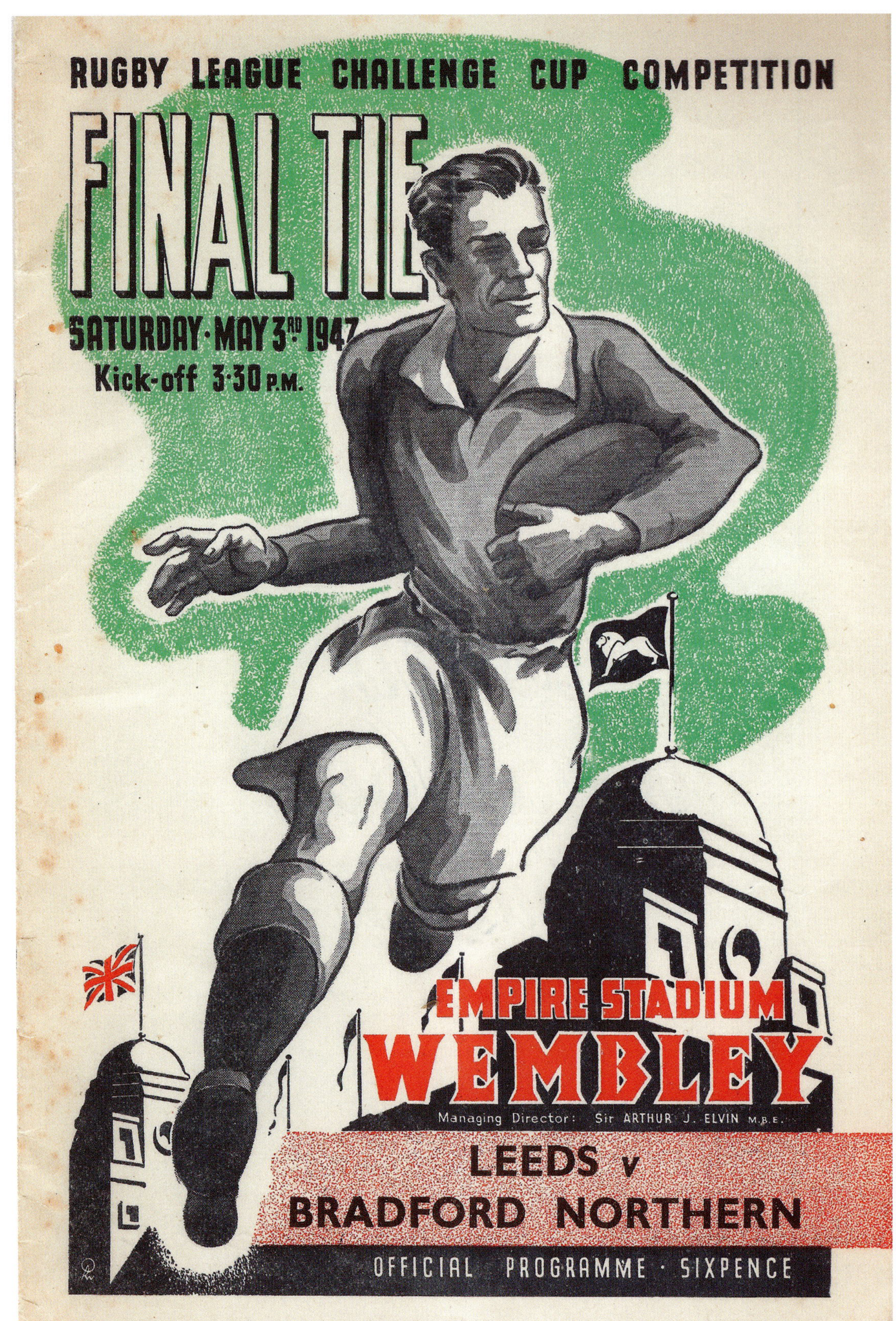

Programme for the 1947 Rugby League Challenge Cup

the Scots side included two midfielders who would become legendary managers, Bill Shankly and Matt Busby. England came out on top with a 3-0 victory.

The unique circumstances led to some unusual bending of rules. Clubs were allowed to use guest players and sometimes reached the wartime finals by using them, only to recall their regular registered players for the Wembley final. This happened to Bill Shankly who never forgave Arsenal, having guested for them en route only to be snubbed for the final. Fellow player Joe Mercer stated that Shankly *was most indignant and his language was dreadful'*. But perhaps the most unusual rule-bending came during the 1943 meeting of England and Wales at Wembley. Stan Mortensen, a member of the England squad who hadn't made the final line-up, found himself making his international debut for the opposition. He had been sitting on the bench in his uniform when early in the game Welsh left-half Ivor Powell sustained a broken collarbone. This reduced Wales to ten men but in a sporting gesture it was agreed at half-time that Mortensen should play for Wales as a substitute. This was still over twenty years before the use of substitutes was officially permitted, but at this time teams would try to have players on stand-by in case some of the team failed to make it, because of the vagaries of wartime transport. In spite of this act of generosity England still went on to win 8-3. Mortensen would go on to complete a proper international debut, and a great deal more. However, he was lucky to have got this far. Having barely survived a crash in a Wellington bomber early in the war, he had initially been told he'd never play again.

The 1945 Wartime League South Cup Final, which was to be the last of this temporary competition, saw Chelsea take the trophy with a 2-0 victory over London rivals, Millwall. While the game generated a healthy £25,000 in gate money, the players only received £2 apiece for their efforts. The King, Queen and Princess Elizabeth were in attendance but didn't witness Chelsea and England forward Tommy Lawton reportedly standing outside the stadium waving his pittance of a payment to passers by shouting *'That's what we get for playing at Wembley'*. He wasn't picked for England for a long while after.

In 1945 Arthur Elvin was honoured with an MBE in recognition of his entrepreneurial work, wartime effort and of course for developing Wembley. This was followed two years later with a knighthood from King George VI. With wartime over, normal sporting service was enthusiastically resumed including speedway and weekly greyhound racing. Whilst a lot else in life was still rationed or in short supply, sport certainly wasn't. It was in these early post-war years that speedway enjoyed its greatest popularity. Wembley Lions fixtures at the stadium would regularly attract crowds in excess of 60,000, with a massive 85,000 for the July match against West Ham. 3rd October 1946 was the biggest crowd of all for Wembley Lions v. Wimbledon when the Lions captain, Bill Kitchen, also demonstrated a rocket-assisted speedway bike designed by a Professor A. M. Low. So many people tried to get in that day that an estimated 20,000 had to be shut outside due to overcrowding. Making the most of its popularity Arthur Elvin set up a Wembley Speedway Supporters Club, which was soon the biggest in the world, boasting a membership of 65,000. Elvin was not exaggerating when he referred to Wembley as the 'Ascot of Speedway', with royalty, politicians and show-business celebrities all part of its vast following.

The first post-war FA Cup Final was between Charlton Athletic and Derby County, and saw the extraordinary feat of Charlton's Bert Turner scoring for both sides in the space of a few minutes. These would be the only goals in normal time but Derby ran out 4-1 winners after extra time, with veteran Raich Carter inspiring his team to score three more through Stamps (twice) and Northern Ireland international Peter Doherty. Charlton manager Jimmy Seed declared afterwards that defeat didn't matter too much as they would be back the following year to lift the cup.

And Seed was true to his word. Charlton did reach the 1947 final where they met Second Division Burnley. The austerity of the time led to some desperate measures. To deck out their heroes out in new football kit, Charlton supporters had pooled ration coupons and bought a new set of shirts for the Cup Final team. Players often had to share and swap football boots in the post-war period due to shortages, and Charlton's Bert Johnson played an hour of the Cup Final with a nail in each boot stabbing into his feet. After the trauma of war such hardships were kept in perspective and a jovial 'Up for the Cup' atmosphere prevailed. Burnley fan John Roberts painted the bonnet of his car in Burnley's claret and blue, drove to Wembley and recalled how he used to fly over the stadium each day as a fighter pilot in the Battle of Britain. As for the final, Charlton did indeed win, courtesy of a Chris Duffy goal in extra-time. In Charlton's post-match celebrations in London's West End the trophy's lid got damaged. After a temporary soldering job by a garage mechanic, it was then properly restored by a silversmith. Continuing in celebratory mood, Jimmy Seed took the cup to his local pub in Mansfield, and passed it round filled with beer.

The 1948 FA Cup Final, between Lancashire rivals Manchester United and Blackpool, was one of the most exciting Wembley had seen. Matt Busby's United had done well to reach the final as, with Old Trafford still undergoing repairs to wartime bomb damage, they had had to play their home cup matches at other grounds in the region. They didn't seem to suffer unduly, producing a fantastic run of results all against First Division opposition. They had relied on spirited teamwork to get them this far, but would it be enough to overcome the brilliant individuals of Blackpool's Mortensen and Matthews and a stubborn defence? In the opening minutes Stan Mortensen was awarded a penalty when he was upended in an offence by Chilton that would, in a later age, have been a straight red card. In an era where centre forwards were allowed to barge goalkeepers, the game was much more of a contact sport. Eddie Shimwell proceeded to score from the spot-kick, only for United to equalise before half time through Rowley. A Stanley Matthews' free kick in the second half was passed

on by Kelly to Mortensen, who regained the lead for the Tangerines. He had scored in every round of the cup that season, becoming the eighth player to achieve the feat. Rowley equalised again, with a diving header, and after a Blackpool surge, United broke to score twice in the last ten minutes through Anderson and Pearson, to take the tie 4-2 and achieve their first Wembley success.

For Bradford Northern, 1948 was the second of what would be three successive Challenge Cup Final visits to Wembley. Having beaten Leeds in 1947, they now came up against Wigan. With BBC television cameras covering the game for the first time, King George VI also became the first reigning monarch to watch a rugby final. Unfortunately, the weather hadn't read the script and the game was played in atrocious conditions. It was a closely fought contest, with Wigan just ahead at half time 5 points to 3. In a very low scoring match, the only three second-half points went to Wigan, giving them an 8-3 victory. Bradford's Frank Whitcombe had the consolation of being named man of the match. At almost 35 he was assuming it might be his Wembley swansong. In fact he was still in the line-up for the final a year later, when another record crowd attended. Bradford Northern's captain Ernest Ward inspired his side to a 13-0 romp over Yorkshire neighbours Halifax – the first time a side failed to score in a Wembley final – with Ward kicking three goals and tries from Batten and Foster.

The 14th Olympiad, the biggest sporting event held since the end of World War Two, began on 29th July 1948 at Wembley Stadium. London had been the intended venue for the 1944 games until war intervened and the games were scrapped, but it had to compete against bids from five other cities. As with much of Europe, the UK was still in financial turmoil and much the same arguments were raised as are today against hosting the games. i.e. that the money should be spent on other priorities – predominantly the rebuilding of areas devastated by bombing. The Games of course went ahead but under the circumstances there could be no such frivolous luxury as a new stadium. Understanding what hosting the games would mean in terms of world coverage, Elvin allowed the Olympic organisers free use of Wembley, and the stadium was transformed for the purpose. Amongst the workforce were German prisoners of war who were employed on roadworks around the stadium, including the construction of Olympic Way leading from Wembley Park station to the twin towers. Inside the stadium, the dirt track that was used for greyhound racing and speedway was dug up and replaced by a cinder running track.

The London Olympics cost £750,000, with track and field athletics, equestrian events and the last two rounds of the football and hockey competitions being held at the stadium, while swimming and diving took place at the neighbouring Empire Pool (now known as Wembley Arena). There was also no such extravagance as an Olympic village for the competitors. Instead they were mainly put up in RAF camps at Uxbridge, West Drayton and Richmond, with male athletes largely separated from the women. Prisoner of War camps were also commandeered, while the PoW's themselves were moved out and put in tents for the duration. Schools, colleges and nursing homes were similarly utilised. Women athletes in the British team were instructed to make their own kits, with just the red and blue bands supplied for the tops. All in all it was a very spartan Olympics, which was perhaps not surprising with food rationing still in force and even more severe than during the war itself. The American team actually brought their own food with them.

As well as being the only two appearances of Charlton Athletic in Wembley FA Cup Finals, the 1946 and 1947 matches were unusual as the ball burst in both games. The poor quality of materials available after the war was seen as the explanation.

The emblem of the 1948 Olympic Games, (by permission of the IOC)

A Cambridge student, John Mark, was given the honour of being the final torch bearer and lighting the Olympic flame – the flame having been carried from Mount Olympia in Greece via a slightly unusual route to steer clear of the civil war on the Greek mainland. King George VI, who as the Duke of York had cut the first turf for the building of Wembley in 1922, opened the games, which were the first to be televised. However, with only around 80,000 households actually owning a television at that time, the BBC's grainy black and white TV coverage was not viewed by many. Echoing the much more sporting spirit of the age, on the large scoreboard inside the stadium was a quote from the founder of the modern Olympic movement, Baron de Coubertin which read, *"The important thing in the Olympic Games is not winning but taking part. The essential thing in life is not conquering but fighting well."*

The Games consisted of 136 events, including the newly introduced women's events of 200 metres, long jump and shot putt. It was also the first Olympics to see the use of starting blocks for track

*John Mark carries the
Olympic Torch for the
1948 London games
(Brent Archive)*

events and the 100 metres final was the first Olympic event ever to be decided by the use of a photo-finish camera. Despite the 'make-do' preparations and at times very poor conditions, 390 women and 3,714 men took part representing 59 countries, which was a record at the time. Nations notable by their absence were Germany, which was not invited, and Japan and the Soviet Union, both of which declined invitations.

The first winner of a major event was the Czech, Emil Zatopek, whose unconventional style served him well in the 10,000 metres. However, the true hero of the London games was 30 year old Dutch mother of two, Francine ('Fanny') Blankers-Koen, who won gold in the 100 metres, 200 metres, 80 metre hurdles and 4x100 metre relay. She actually started the games as record holder in six events but Olympic Games rules limited her to only entering four. Other remarkable performances included 17 year old American Bob Mathias winning the decathlon only four months after taking up the

A poster advertising the 1948 Olympic Games (by permission of the IOC)

The London 1948 games are referred to as the XIV Olympiad (i.e. the 14th) but were only the 11th holding of the modern games. This is because the official numbering includes the three occasions when war prevented the Olympics from actually being held.

sport. He was the youngest athlete in Olympic history to win a men's athletics event and went on to repeat his victory in the Helsinki games four years later. Duncan White of Ceylon (now Sri Lanka) won his country's first ever Olympic medal, coming second in the 400 metre hurdles. Great Britain's Dorothy Tyler won silver in the high jump, a repeat of her achievement in the 1936 Berlin Games. French concert pianist Micheline Ostermeyer won both the shot putt and the discus, while former world champion, Karoly Takacs of Hungary, won the gold for the rapid-fire pistol event having had to learn to shoot left handed after his right hand had been shattered by a grenade.

Day seven of competition featured lacrosse as a demonstration sport at Wembley. There was only one match, which was between England and a New York Polytechnic side that was not actually part of the official USA team. The latter stages of the hockey competition were also played on the Wembley turf with India taking the gold, beating Great Britain in the final, and Pakistan and The Netherlands sharing bronze.

Argentinian Delfo Cabrera took gold in the marathon, overtaking an exhausted and distressed Etienne Gailly of Belgium as they entered the stadium. Gailly came close to passing out as he dramatically struggled to complete the last 400 metres – a lap of the stadium's track – and eventually finished third, also being passed by Britain's Tom Richards who took the silver. Forty-one competitors took part in this eleventh holding of an Olympic marathon, with the race both starting and finishing in the stadium with the route weaving its way through Kingsbury, Stanmore and Elstree.

The USA finished way ahead in the medal table with 38 golds, 27 silver and 19 bronze. Sweden came in second (16 golds), France third (10 golds) followed by Italy, Hungary, Finland, Turkey, Czechoslovakia, Switzerland and The Netherlands. Back in 12th place overall was Great Britain with 3 golds, 12 silver and 6 bronze, which was then the lowest finish by a host nation. Jointly propping up the medal table in 34th place, were Poland, Puerto Rico, Iran and Brazil, each with one bronze.

Following the closing ceremony, which was held at the stadium on the 14th August 1948, all concerned could draw breath and reflect on a great achievement. Even considering Britain's rather indifferent sporting performance and the struggle with preparations and facilities, the holding of the London 1948 games showed unmistakably to the world that London, and Britain as a whole, was truly back in business. Successfully staging such a major event of course greatly raised the profile of Wembley as a venue and added to the prestige of an appearance there. Although the diversity of sport at Wembley would grow, along with the amount of football played there each year, those 17 Olympic days were probably the most intensive use of the stadium in its whole lifespan. It was still to be a slow process but the '48 games can be seen as a turning point in the development of the stadium.

The World Individual Speedway Championship was back at Wembley in 1949 after a ten year absence, and the stadium was packed to the rafters with a 93,000 crowd. It was a triumphant return to Wembley for English speedway as Tommy Price became the first English World Individual Champion and fellow countrymen Jack Parker and Louis Lawson came home in second and third places.

The Liverpool v Arsenal FA Cup Final of 1950 was significant in being the first post war match at Wembley with a crowd of 100,000. Of course, the record breaking crowd of the 1923 FA Cup Final

Finish of the Olympic 110m hurdles, 1948 (Brent Archive)

would never be beaten, but this was the new maximum for the nation's top sporting venue, with crowds having been limited to the low ninety thousands for some time. A 2-0 victory gave the Londoners their third FA Cup win, after a 14 year gap, while for the Merseyside team it was their second cup final defeat. The match was also the final appearance of Arsenal winger, Denis Compton who somehow managed to play at the top level in both football and cricket.

That year's Rugby League Challenge Cup Final saw Australian forward Harry Bath become the first overseas captain to lift the trophy, having led his Warrington side to victory over rivals Widnes by an overwhelming 19-0 score-line. One of the biggest names of Challenge Cup Finals in the early 1950s was Warrington's Phil Jackson, who was also Great Britain captain. He played in two Wembley finals that decade and his comments gave great insight into what players felt on these great occasions: *'It wasn't until later in the game you started to settle down and realised it was just a [rugby] football game. I remember one of the lads, Huey McGregor, was telling me when we first started, his legs wouldn't move with nerves and the open*

Four games from the latter stages of the '48 Olympic Football Competition were held at Wembley, including two featuring that rarity, a Great Britain team. Managed by Matt Busby, Great Britain reached the semi-final where they were defeated by Yugoslavia, and subsequently by Denmark in the Bronze medal play-off. Branislav Stankovic, a Yugoslavian defender, became the first footballer to be sent off at Wembley. Sweden were the eventual winners, beating the Yugoslavs 3-1 in the final.

Programme of the 1948 Rugby League Challenge Cup

spaces and crowd. It's entirely different after being there once. You play better when you get there in later years. I consider myself lucky being able to go three times. Some players play all their career and never get there once.'

The FA had switched their Amateur Cup Final to Wembley in 1949. With there still being a clear distinction between amateur and professional players, the amateur game was held in very high regard. The 1951 Amateur Cup Final attracted a 100,000 crowd, more than the England v. Scotland game a week earlier! That capacity crowd had turned out to see a remarkable 2-1 victory by a now defunct club called Pegasus (after the flying horse from Greek mythology) over Bishop Auckland, who were one of the best amateur sides in the country. The Pegasus victory was extraordinary as the club had only existed for three years, having been set up as a joint venture between Oxford and Cambridge Universities, had no ground of its own and played no regular league fixtures. In contrast, Bishop Auckland, from County Durham, had already won the Amateur Cup seven times. Two years later Pegasus repeated the feat beating Harwich and Parkeston 6-0. Bishop

Auckland were also to return, winning the trophy three times in succession from 1955 to 1957.

The FA Cup Final of '51 saw the first of three Newcastle United victories in five years, all featuring striker Jackie Milburn. The Magpies centre-forward, affectionately known as 'Wor Jackie', scored both goals in a four minute spell to defeat a Blackpool side that included Stanley Matthews and Stan Mortensen. He also became one of a select band of players to score in every round of the cup.

In May 1951, an unbelievable 28 years after the stadium had hosted its first football match, England played their first official international there other than against Scotland. Their opponents for this landmark occasion were Argentina who they had never played before at any venue. Football had been introduced to Argentina by British sailors in Buenos Aires in the 1860s. Clubs from British owned railways companies based there soon sprang up, such as River Plate and Newell's Old Boys, so there were well-established footballing links between the countries. England

Scottish keeper Cowan makes a save in their 3-1 victory over England, April 1949 (© Scottish Football Museum)

came away with a 2-1 victory, but it took two late goals from Stan Mortensen and Jackie Milburn to spare the home side's blushes after the South Americans had taken the lead. Wolves goalkeeper Bert Williams did well to keep the Argentinians at bay, with a performance that some regarded as one of the finest goalkeeping displays ever seen at the stadium.

England had entertained foreign opposition on a number of occasions before but up to that time had used club grounds such as Highbury, White Hart Lane and Goodison Park. From this point on though, Wembley was increasingly used for England games and November '51 saw the first 100,000 crowd for an international beneath the twin-towers when England drew 2-2 with Austria, with goals from Nat Lofthouse and Alf Ramsey.

The referee for the 1952 FA Cup Final, where Newcastle beat Arsenal 1-0, was Arthur Ellis from Halifax. Although this was to be the only Cup Final he would take charge of, he would later find fame as referee on the BBC's bizarre but very popular seventies game show *It's a Knockout* and its Euro-wide version, *'Jeux Sans Frontiere'*. The Prime Minister, Winston Churchill, presented the trophy – the only time a P.M. has done this. The match also saw the start of an unfortunate run of bad injuries to players in FA Cup Finals. That year the unfortunate man was Arsenal's Wally Barnes, who first injured a knee, then tore a cartilage, with his miserable afternoon being completed by Newcastle United's Chilean forward George Robledo heading home a late winner off the post.

Although many a Welshman had trodden the hallowed turf, most notably in Cardiff City's two 1920s FA Cup Finals and two England v Wales unofficial wartime internationals, the first official Welsh national eleven to grace Wembley didn't arrive until November 1952. They possibly wished they hadn't bothered as, despite two goals from Trevor Ford, the team headed back to Wales in dejection, with England putting five past them.

England's goals came courtesy of Nat Lofthouse (2), Tom Finney, Roy Bentley and Jack Froggatt. The Welsh would in fact have to wait another 19 years before so much as a draw at Wembley, and 25 years for a victory.

The FA Cup Final of 1953 brought together two well established top flight clubs, Blackpool and Bolton Wanderers, for what is considered by many to be one of the best ever finals. Despite Bolton scoring early on and having a 3-1 lead well into the second half, Blackpool turned the game round, pulling a goal back in the 68th minute, equalising in the 89th and getting the winner in the 92nd. History has labelled this 'The Matthews Final' after a dazzling performance from the legendary winger, Stanley Matthews. This must have been a great source of frustration to his team-mate, Stan Mortensen who scored three of 'The Tangerines' goals – the first hat-trick in a Cup Final in the 20th Century. However, it was Matthews even at the age of 38 and still an England regular, who had drawn the crowds and lived up to his reputation by endlessly tormenting the Bolton defence. He was a popular national figure and many felt that he had finally got the Cup Winner's medal he deserved, especially after being on the losing side in the '48 and '51 finals. Matthews himself is said to have regarded this as his greatest day.

In spite of the presence of Matthews and Mortensen in the national team, England's footballing pride was to receive a severe dent later that year. In November, the visiting Hungarian national side dubbed 'The Magnificent Magyars' inflicted a bruising 6-3 defeat – England's first loss at Wembley other than to a home nation. Although this was a friendly, such games were taken as seriously as any major competition and for the national side to be so overrun at home was both an embarrassment and a real wake up call. Could it really be that other nations had not only caught up but actually overtaken? The answer was an emphatic 'yes'. The Hungarian side were in the middle of a tremendous run of form that would eventually stretch to 29 games undefeated. They were captained by their own living legend, Ferenc Puskas, from Budapest's Honved Army Team. Nicknamed 'Canoncito' (The Little Canon'), the 26 year old scored two goals that night, and was to lead his nation on to being runners up in the following year's World Cup.

The defeat left English football reeling but, keeping matters in proportion, the Hungarians were almost certainly the best team in the world at that time. England Manager Walter Winterbottom was to hold on to his job for another nine years, however, that game was to be the last England appearance for six of the defeated eleven, including Stan Mortensen and full-back Alf Ramsey, who would turn out to be Winterbottom's ultimate successor. Ramsey's international career as a player had earned him 32 caps, during which time he scored three times – all from penalties and all at Wembley, the last coming in that 6-3 defeat.

At the age of 32, Tom Finney made only his second club appearance at Wembley for Preston North End against West Bromwich Albion in the 1954 Cup Final. As with Stanley Matthews the previous year, most neutrals were rooting for Finney to get the winner's medal his career deserved. However, the man who made a habit of scoring for England and would ultimately play in three World Cups, could not get on the scoresheet. This was not to be 'The Finney Cup Final' as West Brom stole the day with a 3-2 victory. The Preston Plumber, as Finney had been nicknamed for his back-up career plan, remained loyal to his Lancashire club for the whole of his 22 year playing career, but '54 was to be the closest he came to winning club honours.

In November 1954 it was the turn of the 'Gentle Giant' to grace Wembley. John Charles, who went on to be Wales' greatest footballer. After the game he had nothing but praise for the Wembley pitch, describing it as smooth with springy grass, although not easy to play on as you sank into the lush turf as if it were a luxury carpet. You had to *'hit ground passes harder but there was nowhere like it for accuracy of passing. It was as reliable as a snooker table and I loved it.'* Charles' debut went smoothly too, as Ivor Allchurch put him through to score in the 35th minute. Wales might have hung on but with injuries to Ray Daniel (a cut eye) and

Derek Sullivan (knocked unconscious after a clash of heads) they were severely weakened. It was no surprise when England equalised; Roy Bentley scoring from a Stanley Matthews' cross. Bentley then added a second. There was brief joy for Wales when Charles got his second to level the game at two apiece, only for Bentley to go one better and claim a hat-trick, and the winning goal, with seven minutes remaining.

With the international football world clearly evolving, Wembley had to evolve too and floodlights were installed in 1955 ushering in a new era of evening kick-offs. These were used for the first time for a real oddity of a match – a London XI versus a Frankfurt XI in the group stage of the inaugural Inter-Cities Fairs Cup. Although this was later transformed into the more understandable Fairs Cup in the early 1960s and eventually the UEFA Cup, the first bizarre version was played for three years, 1955-58, and was only open to cities that held trade fairs. Only one team was allowed to enter per city, so London entered a representative team selected from a cross-section of London clubs, with a line up that included Bobby Robson, who, 27 years later would become England manager. London were 3-2 winners on the night and eventually went on to reach the final, where they lost to Barcelona. The Frankfurt game was the only one to be staged at Wembley though.

In 1894 Englishman Charles Miller had introduced football to the Brazilian nation with tremendous success. However, it was not until some 62 years later that Brazil's national side came over to play

Miller's descendents. The first England versus Brazil fixture was a friendly match at Wembley on 9th May 1956. Manchester United's Tommy Taylor and Sheffield United's Colin Grainger bagged two apiece as England ran out 4-2 winners, with Paulinho and Didi replying for Brazil. The England side for this auspicious occasion included Wolves' Billy Wright as captain, Blackpool's Stanley Matthews and Fulham's Johnny Haynes.

But despite that magnificent performance, it was an injury to a German ex-Prisoner of War that turned out to be the most enduring Wembley memory of 1956. In the Cup Final, Manchester City were back after defeat the previous year to Newcastle, but this time were to take the trophy back north with them, beating Birmingham City 3-1. The most extraordinary moment came in the 75th minute when Manchester City's German goalkeeper Bert Trautmann dived at the feet of Birmingham striker Murphy. They collided badly, with Murphy's thigh thundering against Trautmann's neck and leaving the City custodian unconscious. Trautmann continued after no more than a rub down with the trainer's magic sponge. He didn't remember much of the rest of the match, collapsing several times in between making some vital saves. He was staggering around the penalty area with one hand supporting his neck, unable to move his head. *It was such a strange sensation. I wasn't seeing any colour – everything around me was grey and I couldn't see any of the players properly. I could only see silhouettes. It was like walking around in fog and trying to find my way*'.

Manchester City held on for a famous win and alongside his team-mates, Trautmann collected his medal from The Duke of Edinburgh in the Royal Box, who asked him if he was in pain. He replied simply that it was a bit like having really bad toothache. It was only four days later that it was found that he'd actually broken his neck making that save. An osteopath at the Manchester Royal Infirmary x-rayed him and discovered he had dislocated five vertebrae in his neck, should have been paralysed and could have died. Having been blamed for the cup final defeat the previous year, the German now found himself a hero and a cup winner to add to being that season's Footballer of the Year.

A year later there was another injury to another Manchester team's goalkeeper. Manchester United had won the league and were hoping to become the first 20th century team to secure the league and cup double. But after just six minutes of play United's Ray Wood collided with Aston Villa's Peter McParland. Concussed, he was replaced in goal by forward Jackie Blanchflower. United held out for a while but in four minutes of mayhem, McParland scored twice – a header and a fierce shot putting Villa two up just before the half hour. Although Wood later staggered back to take over in goal, and Tommy Taylor pulled one back for United, it wasn't enough and the dream of the double was to be over for Busby's Babes.

England's first Wembley defeat to Northern Ireland occurred on 6th November 1957. It was a shock result completely against the run of form and putting an end to England's run of 16 unbeaten match-es. Irish goalkeeper Harry Gregg was man of the match, and goals from Burnley's Jimmy McIlroy, Sammy McCrory of Southend and Bill Simpson of Rangers earned the visitors a 3-2 win.

Recovering from the trauma of '53, a reinvented England side largely restored its dignity in front of Wembley crowds in the latter half of the decade. As well as the win in '56 over Brazil, there was a sound 5-1 defeat over the Republic of Ireland in Wembley's first World Cup Qualifying match, and friendly victories over Portugal, France and the Soviet Union. The Portugal game in May 1958 saw the home England debut of a 20 year old who would go on to become England's highest-ever scorer and to be as well-known worldwide as the stadium itself – Manchester United's Bobby Charlton. His international career very nearly didn't happen, as just three months earlier he'd survived a plane crash that had killed many of his United team mates and several of the team's staff when travel-ling back from a European Cup game via Munich. This warm up game for the forthcoming World Cup in Sweden saw the legend-to-be's international career momentarily overlap with another legend, Tom Finney, in the final months of his. Clearly start-ing the way he meant to go on, Charlton scored both England goals in the 2-1 victory. The 5-0 vic-tory over the Soviets in October that year saw Charlton playing alongside Nat Lofthouse in his last Wembley international appearance. Appropriately, both managed to get on the scoresheet, alongside a hat-trick from Fulham's Johnny Haynes. The game would also turn out to be the final England cap and Wembley appearance of Tom Finney.

In the months following the Munich disaster, Manchester United defied all the odds and reached the 1958 FA Cup Final with a side that now includ-ed several reserves and players playing out of posi-tion, alongside Bobby Charlton. With the whole nation, other than that day's opponents, Lancastrian neighbours Bolton Wanderers, emo-tionally willing them to win, the Reds didn't quite make it a story-book ending, succumbing to two goals from veteran Wanderers' striker, and now captain, Nat Lofthouse.

Playing in England's 1-0 Wembley defeat of Scotland on 11th April 1959, the national side's captain, Billy Wright, became the first footballer in the world to reach 100 caps. To commemorate the occasion he was presented with a silver salver by the Football Association and a two-foot high silver candlestick from the West German FA. His interna-tional career finished later the same year, leaving him with a total of 105 caps.

As the 1950s drew to a close, Wembley was now firmly established as the national football side's regular home venue. With it being the long estab-lished home of football and rugby league cup finals, the list of legends from home and abroad who had graced the turf was now rapidly growing. Sadly, Wembley's owner, Sir Arthur Elvin MBE died in 1957 at the age of 58.

For Wembley, the best years were yet to come and none of it would have been possible had it not been for Sir Arthur Elvin.

The Philip Jackson sculpture of West Ham players Bobby Moore, Geoff Hurst, Martin Peters & Everton's Ray Wilson – all members of the England World Cup team of 1966, near Upton Park, West Ham United's ground

The Wembley of the 1960s was rarely away from centre stage. The slow but sure increase in the stadium's use continued with the England football team playing there more regularly and Wembley's owners experimenting with a range of sporting activities. Most notably the decade would see Wembley in the headlines and on the nation's growing number of TV screens for a series of European club competition finals, a major boxing clash and, biggest of all, the World Cup. Though it could be said that Wembley was already on the map, these were the years when the stadium truly established itself as a great venue for seeing the stars of the day and competitions at the highest level.

April 1961 saw England achieve an astonishing and record breaking 9-3 victory over Scotland in a Home International, including a hat-trick from Chelsea striker Jimmy Greaves. Under the guidance of Walter Winterbottom, a more stable England line-up was in the middle of an impressive run of form. Yet it was still a surprise that the Scots crumpled so badly that day as in their front line was 21 year old Denis Law, who had broken the English transfer record when signing for Manchester City a year earlier, and at the core of their defence was the powerful and dependable Dave MacKay of Spurs. Blame was partly put on the Scots reverting to a selection committee method of choosing the team, and their fear of being seen to select too many 'Anglos' – England based players. The major scapegoat however was the unfortunate Scots goalkeeper, Celtic's Frank Haffey. Enlisted when two more favoured keepers were injured, he was clearly out of his depth and let the occasion get to him. This was only Haffey's second cap, and not surprisingly, his last. After a brief spell at Swindon Town three years later, he emigrated to Australia to develop a new career in comedy, acting and singing.

As if to show that the Scotland match had not been a freak result, England put eight past Mexico without reply in another friendly a month later, this time with a hat-trick from Bobby Charlton, now a regular fixture in the England side. Also scoring against both Scotland and Mexico was a young Bobby Robson with what would turn out to be the last of the four goals of his international career. Even after such victories though, there was little in the way of post-match extravagance. Robson, for example, travelled back home to the Midlands by bus and train. Players' travel expenses at the time were dealt with by the team manager, Walter Winterbottom, and didn't extend to taxis.

Three weeks after a match he'd probably rather forget, Dave Mackay returned to Wembley for happier times with Tottenham Hotspur. Captained by their 35 year old Northern Ireland international, Danny Blanchflower, Spurs beat Leicester City 2-0 in the FA Cup Final of 1961, to complete the first League and Cup 'double' of the 20th century, and the first of their three Cup wins in the decade. A quarter of an hour had elapsed when Leicester right back Len Chalmers suffered a knee ligament injury but limped on. Bobby Smith latched onto a Terry Dyson through ball in the 69th minute to put Spurs one up. The double was clinched on 77 minutes when Smith crossed and Dyson headed home. Unfortunately for Leicester, this was the first of three Cup Final defeats in the sixties. However, in their otherwise fairly undistinguished line-up that day were a young goalkeeper, Gordon Banks, in his pre-England days, and young half-back, Frank McLintock who would lift the Cup as Arsenal captain some ten years later.

In May 1963 Wakefield Trinity achieved their third win in four years of the Rugby League Challenge Cup, defeating Wigan 25-10 in the Final. That victory was probably the most dramatic of the three, as despite the '60 and '62 wins they were very much considered the underdogs. Man of the day was Trinity's stand-off Harold Poynton. Late in the second half with Trinity only five points ahead, he made a vital interception during a Wigan attack and raced down the other end for a try, effectively finishing off the game.

Olympic Way (also known as Wembley Way), early 1960s (Brent Archive)

Gordon Banks, generally considered to be the greatest goalkeeper of all time, made his England debut at Wembley against Scotland in April 1963. Scottish legend Jim Baxter scored twice against a Bryan Douglas reply to send the Tartan Army into rapture. As it had been in the past (and was to continue to be in the future) the Scots' support out-sang and seemed to outnumber the home crowd. Baxter played the game of his life, rampaging down the left wing and humiliating the English defence by playing 'keepy uppy'. At the final whistle he stuffed the match ball up his jersey and justifiably swaggered off the pitch.

Another British legend saw his first sight of Wembley in 1963. George Best was just sixteen and had been told by Matt Busby he was to be signed up as a first team player. His Manchester United team-mates had reached the FA Cup Final, against Gordon Banks' Leicester City. Although he wasn't selected to play, Best was on the team bus to Wembley accompanied by his father. He later reflected on his inaugural Wembley visit that *'the first team lads just about demolished Leicester… …the atmosphere was electric. It was my first trip to Wembley and I appreciated immediately just what it was that made Cup Final day different to anything else in that mighty stadium'*.

The stadium itself continued to be improved and modernised with the addition of a much fuller glass and aluminium roof and an electronic scoreboard added in 1963, at a cost of £500,000. This was in preparation for a highly prestigious first for the venue – the hosting of that year's final of the European Cup, the competition that later evolved into the Champions League. Italy's Milan took on Portugal's Benfica attempting to win the trophy for the third year in succession. In this pre-Champions League era, when TV coverage of European football was much rarer, such a clash of giants really was an occasion to be savoured. Despite the presence in the Benfica side of Eusebio, probably the greatest player Portugal has ever produced, the Italian side came out on top, winning 2-1.

Just a few weeks later, for one heady Tuesday evening in June, the stadium turned its attention to boxing for the first time since 1924. Britain's heavyweight champion, Henry Cooper, took on the American, Cassius Clay, eight years his junior, later

known to the world as Muhammad Ali. Only 21 years old, and known as much for his talent for self-promotion as for his boxing skill, Clay was rapidly becoming the most famous boxer on the planet. The fight poster billed him as 'The World's Greatest Showman', though there was no doubting he had the ability to back up his words. With the ring set up in the middle of the pitch, a crowd of around 40,000 watched the fight live, paying from twelve shillings and sixpence (60p) to six guinea's (£6.60) for a ringside seat. Scheduled for ten rounds, this eliminator for the Heavyweight Championship of the World was over in five, with Clay winning by a knockout. It had nearly been very different. In the fourth round a Cooper left hook had floored Clay, who had to take a count for the first time in a professional bout. With the bell ringing for the end of the round as Clay was getting back to his feet, he had time to draw breath and regain his composure between rounds. Many believe that it's this that saved the American from a shock first defeat. 'Our Enry' maintained a Wembley connection through his greengrocer's shop on Ealing Road, near Wembley High Street. Throughout the 1960s, he would often work there with his twin brother, serving fruit and vegetables.

In a match marking the hundredth anniversary of

Programme from the Cooper versus Clay fight 1963

the Football Association, England took on a Rest of the World XI in October '63. Goals from Terry Paine and Jimmy Greaves gave the hosts a 2-1 victory over a side that included Portugal's Eusebio, Scotland's Denis Law and the veteran Spanish centre-forward Alfredo Di Stefano, who had led Real Madrid to five consecutive European Cup wins. Just four weeks later, in the first international match to be played under floodlights, a crowd of 55,000 watched England embarrass Northern Ireland 8-3 in a Home International. Greaves was back on the scoresheet, this time with four goals, while Terry Paine scored a hat-trick.

> Whereas the Wembley Lions speedway fixtures were graciously switched to other tracks for the length of the World Cup, Wembley's owner refused to cancel a greyhound meeting which clashed with the Group One match between Mexico and Uruguay. The game instead took place a few miles away at the White City Stadium in Shepherds Bush, West London.

On a May afternoon a young team captain, Bobby Moore, found himself climbing the 39 steps up to Wembley's Royal Box to be presented with a trophy at Wembley. It was the 1964 F.A. Cup Final, in which West Ham defeated Preston North End 3-2. It was a task Moore that was to become very familiar with. The Cup Final victory qualified the Hammers for the following season's European Cup Winner's Cup. Casting aside opposition from Belgian, Czech, Swiss and Spanish clubs, they reached the final, which as fate would have it, was that season at Wembley. Though considered less prestigious than the European Cup (and later merged with the UEFA Cup) no side would have turned down the chance of some European glory. In the final West Ham met the West German side TSV München 1860, and came away with a 2-0 victory, both goals coming from their 23 year old reserve outside-right, Alan Sealey. Geoff Hurst said of the match, *'That was probably West Ham's greatest performance…everything we had worked at and tried over the past two or three years clicked into place. It was a marvellous sense of achievement to win on that May evening, watched by 100,000 spectators at Wembley and goodness knows how many millions of people on television throughout Europe.'*

Little did they know it but for three of the Hammers line-up that night, Moore, Hurst and Peters, even this triumph was just a trial run for greater glory still over German opposition at Wembley a year later.

The 1966 FA Cup Final was inevitably overshadowed in history by the football events that took place later that summer. However it produced one of the greatest Cup Final comebacks. Everton were up against Sheffield Wednesday, and the Yorkshire side soon went into a comfortable 2-0 lead. Everton's Cornishman Mike Trebilcock, a fringe team player who hadn't even warranted a mention in the match day programme, led a dramatic turnaround. He scored twice before Derek Temple grabbed a winner for the Merseysiders. Left back Ray Wilson collected his winner's medal little realising that two months later he would be back in the Royal Box as a World Cup winner, becoming the only Englishman to win both medals in the same season.

In the '50s and '60s players picked up bad injuries all too frequently playing on 'the hallowed turf' and several Cup Finals were spoilt as a contest when one team was reduced to ten men. This became known as 'The Wembley Hoodoo' and led to the introduction of substitutes in the domestic game in 1965. Initially just one sub was allowed per side – a situation that's hard to imagine in these days of multiple substitutions, and even entire teams being replaced for the second halves of international friendlies.

The main sporting event of the decade was England's hosting and winning of the 1966 World Cup. Venues all over the country were used but Wembley was very much the centrepiece, staging nine games including all of England's. This was the first and, so far, the only time that the competition has come home to the nation that invented football. Even so England had had to fight off rival bids from Spain and West Germany. Fourteen nations came through qualification to join England as hosts and Brazil as holders, having won in Chile in '62. As they hadn't had to go through a qualifying group England had not played many genuinely competitive games in the build up. Nevertheless, the friendlies they had played had gone exceptionally well, and the side went into battle this time on a wave of confidence having been unbeaten in their previous ten games.

With the benefit of decades of hindsight it's all too easy to believe that England went into the finals with a well established world-beating side but it wasn't quite so clear cut at the time. The squad could boast Bobby Moore as captain, along with Jimmy Greaves, Bobby Charlton and Ray Wilson, all survivors from the '62 World Cup squad, but this was a team still in transition – even three and a half years after the sacking of Walter Winterbottom who had led England to very poor World Cup campaigns in '58 and '62. Having managed Ipswich Town for seven years and taken them from the Third to the First Division, Alf Ramsey had taken over the reigns of the national side at the end of '62 and ushered in a very new era. Firstly, as a condition of taking the job he demanded sole charge of team selection, which had up to that point been done by the FA's International Committee.

Then, after only one game in charge, Ramsey cast

The 1966 World Cup was the first to have an official mascot – a footballing cartoon lion named 'World Cup Willie'. England's campaign was accompanied by an irrepressibly jolly song of the same name, sung by the 'King of Skiffle', Lonnie Donegan – a Scotsman! It failed to reach the charts.

aside regular keeper, Sheffield Wednesday's Ron Springett, and drafted in Leicester City's number one, Gordon Banks – a decision that was already paying dividends. Much of the rest of the squad was less established, however, and met with a lot of criticism, in particular the selection of centre-half Jack Charlton, Bobby's older brother, then 32. Everton's teenage star, Alan Ball had only made his England debut the previous year, and the West Ham duo of Geoff Hurst and Martin Peters had only graduated to the England side earlier in '66. So whilst Ramsey was unshakably confident and had already boldly forecast that England would win the World Cup, many of the squad were relatively untested at the top level. Ramsey was also responsible for introducing much greater discipline and the radical new 4-3-3 formation. This abandoned the use of conventional wingers, leading to his team being dubbed the 'wingless wonders'. It had only been tried by Ramsey in England's handful of warm up games but with great success.

Playing all three of their Group One games at Wembley, England got the tournament under way on the 11th July 1966 with a disappointing 0-0 draw against Uruguay. Subsequent victories against Mexico and France however meant that they topped their group, and in doing so, kept themselves at Wembley. Hurst didn't feature at all in the group stage with Greaves being preferred. In one of those twists of fate, however, Greaves picked up an injury in the France game, leaving the door open for Hurst to move into the spotlight.

The quarter-final pitted England against Argentina. This most infamous of clashes – and clash really is the appropriate word – is best remembered for the appalling tackling and behaviour of the Argentinians, which culminated in their captain,

The Programme of the 1966 World Cup Final (Brent Archive)

Rattin, being sent off but refusing to leave the field for almost ten minutes. And that was just the first half. In the second, despite their man advantage, England struggled until late on when, as if scripted, Peters crossed for Hurst to put away the goal to send a relieved England into the semi-finals. Ramsey prevented his players from exchanging shirts at the final whistle and afterwards angrily described the Argentinians as 'animals'.

A mere three days later, England faced Eusebio and his Portugal side, who had already contributed to putting the Brazilians out of the tournament. With Brazil's Pelé heading home early it was Eusebio who captured the imagination of the public, and was also ultimately the top scorer for the tournament with a total of nine. However in this meeting, a thunderbolt goal in each half from Bobby Charlton saw England through. Despite a late goal from Eusebio and tremendous pressure in the dying minutes, it was the Portuguese star who left the pitch in tears as the home nation celebrated reaching its first ever World Cup Final.

The 1966 World Cup Final took place on 30th July before a crowd of 96,924 and what's believed to be the highest British TV audience ever – 32.3 million. A remarkable feat considering there were only 15 million households with TV sets at that time. More incredible still is that an estimated 600 million are believed to either have watched TV coverage or listened to radio commentary worldwide. England played in their second strip of red shirts, white shorts and West Germany in their usual white shirts and black shorts. Ramsey kept the faith with the eleven who had safely navigated England through the quarter and semi finals, which was a decision that would be to the eternal disappointment of Jimmy Greaves, as it meant that Geoff Hurst kept his place in the side ahead of him. The Germans were captained by 29 year old Uwe Seeler, playing in his third consecutive World Cup Finals. The team also featured the rising star of German football, a young midfielder from Bayern Munich, Franz Beckenbauer.

It was the Germans who went ahead early on when Helmut Haller took advantage of a rare mistake from Ray Wilson in the 13th minute. England levelled just six minutes later with Hurst, finding himself in acres of space, heading home a quickly

taken free kick from Moore. A series of excellent saves by Banks kept the Germans at bay and the scores remained level until the 77th minute when Martin Peters fired home the loose ball from seven yards after a shot from Hurst was deflected across the penalty box. For the next twelve minutes, which must have seemed like an eternity to Peters, he would be the man who'd scored the goal to win England the World Cup. In the last minute however, Jack Charlton gave away a free-kick 25 yards out. To the disbelief of a watching nation, the ball was played into the English penalty area, and Wolfgang Weber pulled a goal back to make it 2-2 forcing the game into extra-time. Replays later revealed that England had a legitimate claim for hand-ball in the scramble that led to the goal. Banks can clearly be seen immediately appealing. But extra-time it was.

Ten minutes into the first extra period, Hurst struck the ball against the German crossbar. It rocketed down behind 'keeper Tilkowski, on or perhaps just over the line, for what has become one of the most analysed goal-line decisions in footballing history. After lengthy discussions with the 'Russian' linesman, Tofik Bakhramov, the goal was given. Although it has been disputed ever since, and with some justification, as with any decision, once it's made, it stands and players simply have to get on with the game. The contest effectively seemed over as England coped admirably with the last attacks of a drained German team through the second period

World Cup Willie, the 1966 England World Cup mascot. (by permission of The Football Asscociation)

of extra-time. Then with seconds left, Moore hit a 35 yard pass forward to Hurst, who surged into the opposing penalty area. As a few spectators began to spill onto the pitch thinking the final whistle had already gone, Hurst struck the ball decisively past a despairing Tilkowski to complete a 4-2 victory and the only hat-trick ever scored in a World Cup Final.

Moore led the team up to receive the Jules Rimet Trophy from the Queen, and with it the undying respect of the nation. The players all received a bonus of £1,000 on top of their £60 match fee. A £6,000 bonus went to manager Alf Ramsey who would later also receive a knighthood, and all three match officials received golden whistles from the Queen. On the wave of euphoria that followed, Labour Prime Minister Harold Wilson, who had just gambled on an early General Election, winning with an increased parliamentary majority, boasted that host nations often seem to win under socialist/labour governments. Mind you, fortunes for himself and England were to reverse in 1970.

A sculpture of Moore will take pride of place in Olympic Way (also known as Wembley Way) – the main route for fans as they approach the new Wembley Stadium from Wembley Park tube station. The work was produced by Philip Jackson who also created the sculpture close to Upton Park of Moore holding the World Cup aloft, held by his team-mates after the '66 triumph.

While the early '60s had seen Britain finally re-emerging from the rationing and reconstruction of the post-war era – the austerity years – in the second half of the decade a newly confident, vibrant, creative nation appeared, appropriately enough coinciding with the beginnings of colour TV. To a soundtrack of The Beatles, The Rolling Stones and The Kinks, Britain – and London in particular – was fast becoming the place to be for music and fashion, and for sportsmen Wembley was the ultimate stage to be seen on. The rapid growth in ownership of TV sets, 8 out of 10 households in Britain by the end of the decade, allowed our sporting heroes to be seen ever more widely. Fuelled by this and the flamboyance and expression of the new generation, as the decade progressed, we also witnessed the beginnings of a new phenomenon – footballers with almost pop-star like status.

In a move to improve the image and prestige of the competition, the Football League Cup Final was played at Wembley and on a Saturday for the first time in 1967. Created by Alan Hardaker, the Secretary of the Football League, for the previous five seasons of its existence, the final had been played over two legs and had only attracted small crowds. More to the point, the competition had so far failed to regularly attract the participation of the top clubs. In an excellent advert for the competition Queens Park Rangers, at that point runaway leaders of the Third Division, came up against Division One side and cup holders, West Bromwich Albion. West Brom seemed to have the game sewn up tak-

The 'Russian Linesman' of the '66 World Cup Final, Mr Bakhramov, should more accurately be referred to as the 'Soviet' linesman. He was actually from the city of Baku in Azerbaijan, which was then part of the Soviet Union. He died in 1993 at the age of 67 but has been honoured by his home city, with the national stadium being named after him and more recently with a statue of him unveiled in 2004 by none other than... Geoff Hurst.

ing a 2-0 lead into half-time but QPR, featuring Rodney Marsh, scored three second half goals to steal victory. The following two seasons saw successive defeats for Arsenal, losing 1-0 to Leeds United in '68, and worse still, 3-1 in extra-time to Third Division Swindon Town the following year. The game was played on one of those abysmal mud and sand pitches that wouldn't be considered acceptable today, having not recovered from recent games and heavy rain. That day, however, belonged to Don Rogers, scoring once in each period of extra-time for the west country side. Whilst it was a shock defeat for 'The Gunners' all but a couple of the side that day would be around for the side's domestic and European successes in the following seasons. Arsenal's traumas aside, for the competition as a whole though, the switch to Wembley had been a tremendous success with near capacity crowds for the finals and the top clubs now seeing the light. It has to be said that the added incentive of a place in Europe, in the Fairs Cup, probably had something to do with it.

Scotland gained a much needed boost to their national pride in April '67 beating England, the World Champions, 3-2 in their own backyard. Now under the management of Bobby Brown, the Scots arrived full of confidence and not afraid to show their style and flair against an England side that contained ten of the eleven who'd defeated West Germany, and gone an extraordinary 19 games unbeaten. Denis Law, a survivor from the 9-3 humiliation, was back with a vengeance. Now with Manchester United and scoring an average of over 20 goals a season, he was at the peak of his pow-

ers and, sure enough, was first on the scoresheet. It wasn't until the second half that Bobby Lennox put the Scots two ahead but instead of this finishing the game off, it only brought on a frantic climax of three goals in the final five minutes. Jackie Charlton pulled one back for the home side, McCalliog then restored the two goal margin and finally Hurst got

Programme for the League Cup Final 1967

a late header to make the game look closer than it had really been. Scottish fans couldn't contain their pleasure at the victory and invaded the pitch at the end. But after all, beating the World Cup holders meant that they could, for short time at least, claim to be the best in the world! To commemorate the event, many pieces of Wembley turf were 'borrowed' for gardens and window boxes north of the border. Although part of the Home International Championship, that year's tournament also doubled as a qualifying group for the European Nations Cup. Despite the Scots victory it wasn't enough and ultimately England would qualify. A crystal ball would have brought further solace to the English, as it would be fully ten years before the Scots would get their next win at Wembley.

The third round of Bobby Charlton versus Eusebio took place in May '68, with the return of the European Cup Final to Wembley, and Manchester United taking on Benfica from Portugal. Although Eusebio almost snatched a winner at the end of normal time, with the scores at 1-1 this was to be

a fourth unhappy visit to the twin-towers for the Portuguese star. That hot May night, it was United's stars that shone brightest. George Best put United ahead in extra-time in what is considered to be the high point of his career, with Brian Kidd and Bobby Charlton then putting the game beyond the Lisbon club. Just ten years after many of the Old Trafford side had died in the Munich air crash, the team, rebuilt by manager Matt Busby, became the first English club to win the European Cup. England as a whole celebrated this achievement, with many putting aside the usual club rivalries, and Busby was later knighted for his services to football. As well as the capacity Wembley crowd of 100,000, it's estimated that a TV audience of 250 million watched the game worldwide.

In July 1968 show jumping returned to Wembley for the first time since the 1948 Olympics. For a week the stadium hosted a variety of competitions in the Royal International Horse Show. The event failed to pull in the crowds however, despite the appearance of top equestrian stars including Britain's David Broome. The terrible damage the horses' hooves inflicted on the pitch was to prove a big problem too and after just one further year the event moved on to pastures new.

1970-1979: Pop Stars, Perms & Broken Crossbars 5

The Seventies was a period when the 'Grand Old Lady', as the stadium was sometimes called, branched out into exciting and prosperous new ventures. The sound of music reverberating around the ground had previously only come courtesy of military bands in pre-match entertainment but live acts from the pop and rock world started to view the stadium as a potential venue. Meanwhile, the annual showpiece football and rugby finals went from strength to strength, boosted by global television coverage and the spread of colour TV. But while the domestic game was overflowing with talent, flair and character, England's football fortunes waned dramatically, as Fortress Wembley was breached by more countries than ever before. Despite, or maybe because of, trying four different managers at the helm, the national team was rarely able to reproduce the form of bygone years.

The first major event of 1970 was the League Cup Final which was another muddy affair. FA Cup holders Manchester City faced the 1968 FA Cup and 1966 League Cup winners, West Bromwich Albion. City went into the match exhausted from having played the away leg of a European Cup Winners' Cup Quarter Final in Portugal on the Wednesday. Their flight back to London to prepare for the Wembley final was diverted to Birmingham because of snow, and they finally arrived by coach at their Wembley hotel in the small hours of Friday morning. As seemed to be the norm for the League Cup, with the slightest hint of a colour clash both teams opted to wear their second strips – red and black stripes for City, and all white for Albion. The match started well for Albion with Jeff Astle (who was to feature in England's World Cup campaign in Mexico a few months later) heading the opening goal after just five minutes. Mike Doyle equalised in the 60th minute and the match went into extra time. Francis Lee, the one City player to overcome fatigue, crossed for Glyn Pardoe to score the winner. City captain Tony Book commented that *'On a Wembley pitch that was in a sorry state and resembled a mud-flat, Frannie Lee rose to the heights, an*

Everest of a performance and quite the best I that I have ever seen.' These were halcyon days for Manchester City, who two months later became the third English team to lift the European Cup Winners Cup.

That year's FA Cup Final was held on 11th April, the earliest in the season it had ever been held. The intention had been to give World Cup holders England maximum preparation time to defend their title in Mexico, but it resulted in a serious fixture pile up for some clubs. Leeds United and Chelsea tried to perform on a muddy and heavily sanded pitch, producing a spectacle far removed from the traditional FA Cup Final usually held on a green baize-like surface under May sunshine. It made life very awkward for defenders and goalkeepers with unpredictable or non-existent bounces. Leeds twice went ahead through Jack Charlton and Mick Jones, only to be pegged back both times, the Chelsea goals provided by Peter Houseman and Ian Hutchinson. Even extra-time couldn't separate the sides, leaving a result that also broke with tradition; the 2-2 score-line being the first-ever draw in a Wembley FA Cup Final. The replay at Old Trafford saw Chelsea win 2-1 in extra time, with David Webb scoring the winner, and making amends for his torrid two hours in the Wembley match against Eddie Gray's wing wizardry.

The only Wembley Home International of the year took place on 21st April, and was a 3-1 victory for England over Northern Ireland. A capacity crowd applauded as Bobby Charlton was made captain for the match to honour his becoming only the second Englishman to win one hundred caps. The FA presented him with a silver salver displaying flags of FIFA and the thirty countries that he had played against to earn his century of caps. He went on to reach 106 caps, beating Billy Wright's total by one. George Best did his best to spoil the party for his Manchester United team-mate, scoring Northern Ireland's only goal that night and what was to prove to be his only international goal at Wembley. Later that year, goalkeeper Peter Shilton

Programme for the 1970 FA Cup Final

made his full England debut in a 3-1 win over East Germany – the start of an international career that was to last a remarkable 20 years.

Skelmersdale United's 4-1 defeat of Dagenham in the April 1971 FA Amateur Cup Final was a tremendous success for the Lancashire non-leaguers. But the aftermath of the match was to have big implications and ultimately sound the death knell for the amateur game. It was an open secret that many supposedly amateur players were actually paid one way or another, and in some cases more than the players of semi-professional clubs. Shortly after the Wembley final, Skelmersdale's manager is reported as saying that 'shamateurism' (as it had become known) was everywhere, and that the richest clubs had to pay for their success. As if to emphasise that the distinction between professional and amateur was very blurred if not entirely gone, his club turned professional immediately after the Dagenham game. This issue was something that the footballing authorities had been hoping would go away if they ignored it, and it was two more years before the nettle was grasped and the Amateur Cup was scrapped. The now futile attempt to distinguish between professional and amateur was abandoned. Now there were simply 'players'. The FA Trophy had already been introduced in 1970 for all non-league clubs but now the FA Vase competition was also created, effectively in place of the Amateur Cup, for the lower levels of non-league football. Both competitions carried the incentive of a prestigious Wembley final.

The 1971 FA Cup Final saw Bertie Mee's Arsenal overcome the legendary Bill Shankly's Liverpool in a thrilling extra time battle. After ninety minutes in the blazing sunshine neither side had managed to score. Liverpool took the lead in the first minute of extra time through Steve Heighway but Arsenal soon levelled the scores with an odd equaliser after George Graham's shot brushed the leg of team-mate Eddie Kelly and went in, making Kelly the first substitute to score in a Cup Final. With their strength sapped, Liverpool were finally undone by precocious Highbury hero Charlie George. With his socks rolled down and long hair flowing, he rifled in a 25 yard winner in the 111th minute, before collapsing on his back, arms aloft awaiting the acclaim of his team-mates. Shankly's team are said to have blamed their defeat partly on their long sleeved shirts being made of too heavy a material. But be it shirts, stamina or skill, Arsenal's yellow and blue short-sleeved eleven won the day. The Gunners had also been in action the previous Monday night, clinching the League Championship title at Tottenham of all places. So with their Wembley victory, Mee's side, with captain Frank McLintock and goalkeeper Bob Wilson (now a sports presenter) emulated their North London rival's League and Cup Double achievement of ten year's previous.

In rugby league, the Challenge Cup Final of that year saw underdogs Leigh defeat Leeds 24-7. With fifteen minutes remaining Leeds centre and captain Syd Hynes became the first player to be sent off in a Wembley Challenge Cup final. This for allegedly head-butting Leigh scrum-half and captain Alex Murphy. The unconscious Murphy was carried off on a stretcher and took no further part in the game. After treatment in the dressing room, however he was able to return to the field to watch the last five minutes, receive his medal and join the lap of honour. Hynes later suggested that it had been a faked injury. However, as the TV cameras missed the incident, we shall never know. Murphy was also named as Man of the Match for his two goals and inspirational leadership that day. A rugby league and Wembley legend, he had also won the Challenge Cup with St Helens in 1961 and 1966 and would be back as player-coach with Warrington in 1974.

The most prestigious European club match, the European Cup Final, would be hosted by Wembley twice in the 1970s. In 1971, the Johann Cruyff-inspired Dutch masters, Ajax Amsterdam, ran out 2-0 winners over Greek hopefuls Panathinaikos, managed by Hungarian legend Ferenc Puskas. Against an Ajax side packed with internationals and their seemingly unbeatable 'Total Football' style, the Athens club never really stood a chance, although it was nevertheless the greatest achievement of Greek football to date. But this was an Ajax side at its peak, forming the backbone of the Dutch national side, and on its way to three consecutive European Cup wins.

A landmark event for Stoke City fans took place in March 1972 when The Potters finally won a trophy after 109 years of trying. The second oldest club in the Football League (after Notts County) celebrated as 36 year old veteran George Eastham scored the winner in a 2-1 League Cup victory over Chelsea. It was a match packed with British international players and star players of the era. Stoke City lined up with Gordon Banks in goal, a defence of John Marsh, Dennis Smith, Alan Bloor and Mike Pejic; Jimmy Greenhoff, Peter Dobing and George Eastham in midfield, with John Ritchie and Terry Conroy up front. Welsh international John Mahoney came on as a substitute. Chelsea had reserve keeper Paddy Mulligan in goal; Ron 'Chopper' Harris, John Dempsey and David Webb in defence, John Hollins, Charlie Cooke, Alan Hudson and Peter Houseman in midfield and Chris Garland and Peter Osgood in attack.

Having won their qualifying group against quite weak opposition from Malta, Greece and Switzerland during the previous year, England faced the West Germans in the first leg of a European Nations Cup Quarter-Final at the end of April '72. The Germans had already got their revenge for '66 in the Mexico World Cup, but Franz Beckenbauer and his side were to make England pay again. A goal in the 27th minute from Uli Höeness separated the sides until a Francis Lee equaliser in the 78th raised English hopes. But late goals from Günter Netzer and 'Der Bomber' Gerd Müller meant that the Germans left with a 3-1 advantage. The return leg two weeks later in Berlin ended 0-0 leaving England the losers on aggregate, while the West Germans went on to win the competition. To rub salt into English wounds a few weeks later in May, England surprisingly suffered only their second Wembley defeat by Northern Ireland. A 34th minute goal by player-manager Terry Neill decided the match, along with two great saves from Pat Jennings which denied Rodney Marsh.

Large outdoor music festivals had taken off in the UK in the late 1960s and early 1970s with Hyde Park, the Isle of Wight Festival and the early Glastonburys setting the tone for the future of rock music. Although the neighbouring Empire Pool had long hosted concerts, the stadium set a precedent for a musical future with its first gig in August 1972. This was 'The London Rock and Roll Show' which starred Little Richard and Chuck Berry. Also on the bill were Bill Haley and the Comets, Jerry Lee Lewis, Bo Diddley and Roy Wood's Wizard.

1972 was a mixed year for speedway at Wembley. The downside was that the Wembley Lions

Arsenal's 1971 FA Cup Final win as portrayed by Scorcher 'n' Score comic that year (by permission of Egmont UK Ltd)

dropped out of the top division and put their racing licence on hold. However, in the global arena, the World Championship was well attended with an 80,000 crowd. Legendary New Zealander, Ivan Mauger, who had won his first Wembley world title in 1969, was amongst the favourites in 1972. Four-time champion and fellow Kiwi, Barry Briggs was another of the favourites. However, tragedy was to strike him in heat five when he fell from his bike and was accidentally hit by the fast approaching Valeri Gordeev. Briggs was immediately taken to hospital and had to have a finger amputated. Back at the track, the final was as close as could be, with underdog Bernt Person pushing Mauger to the wire. They finished with equal points but in the run-off it was Mauger who claimed victory and his second Wembley World Championship, and his fourth overall. Dane Ole Olsen finished third that year but would be back to improve on that by winning the next two championships to be held at Wembley, in 1975 and 1978, pipping White City Rebels' Gordon Kennett to the title in the latter, by just one point.

An attempt to mix sport and politics came to the Twin Towers in January '73. With the UK, Denmark and the Republic of Ireland all joining the European Economic Community, a rather pointless celebratory match was contrived between 'The Three' (those joining the EEC) and 'The Six' (those already in), with the new kids on the EEC block coming out 2-0 winners. A crowd of 36,000 turned out on a winters day to witness the star-studded line-ups with the likes of Bobby Charlton, Bobby Moore, Emlyn Hughes and Pat Jennings on display for 'The Three', while Italian goalkeeper Dino Zoff, German legends Franz Beckenbauer, Gerd Müller and Günter Netzer and Dutch stars Rudi Krol and Johan Neeskens turned out for 'The Six'.

Wales held England to a 1-1 draw in January 1973 in their three-team World Cup qualification group (also including Poland) – a result that was to have serious consequences for England later in the year. Making their first Wembley international appearances that night in the home side's line-up were Liverpool winger Kevin Keegan and goalkeeper Ray Clemence, both of whom would go on to have long and successful careers for club and country. Conversely, for Manchester City's striker Rodney

Marsh, this was to be a disappointing end to his England career, gaining his ninth and last cap.

The FA Cup Final of 1973 saw surprise Division Two package, Sunderland, facing cup holders Leeds United, in what proved to be the decade's most talked about final. Don Revie's Yorkshiremen were a dominant force in the league and with a regular starting eleven of British and Irish internationals including captain Billy Bremner and centre-back Norman 'bites yer legs' Hunter, they were expected to make light work of the Black Cats. In a Wembley game also notable for the rare use of a pale orange ball, a first half goal from Scottish number ten Ian Porterfield put the underdogs ahead. Sunderland's goalkeeper, Jim Montgomery pulled off a string of spectacular stops as they soaked up immense pressure from Leeds. The most memorable being an incredible double save from a Trevor Cherry header followed up by Peter 'hot-shot' Lorimer which somehow Montgomery turned on to the crossbar. They held onto their lead for the rest of the ninety minutes and on the final whistle Sunderland manager Bob Stokoe, attired in a trilby hat, beige raincoat and red track-suit bottoms, danced a jig of joy on the pitch and hugged Montgomery. Minutes later captain Bobby Kerr climbed the 39 steps to the Royal Box to receive the famous trophy.

A week later, the Challenge Cup Final of '73 also had a shock winner as Featherstone Rovers beat Bradford Northern by 33 points to 14. Star performer was veteran full back Cyril Kellett, who weighed in with eight goals – a Wembley record – although the Man of the Match Award went to Rover's local boy and Great Britain international, half back Steve Nash. A year later, Featherstone were back to defend their crown, only to go down 24-9 at the hands of Warrington. Despite being ahead at half-time, in a rather disjointed game, Rover's bubble was burst by the boot of full-back Derek Whitehead who kicked seven goals.

In October 1973 there was a less pleasant shock for the Wembley crowd. After the January draw with Wales and a subsequent loss away to Poland, England were left needing to win when the Poles visited Wembley, in order to qualify for the 1974 World Cup in West Germany. After a goalless first half, Jan Domarski dismayed the home crowd by putting Poland ahead in the 55th minute. Alan

Clarke levelled from the penalty spot just eight minutes later but it would not be enough. Although England gallantly peppered the Polish goal with shots, the game was to finish as a 1-1 draw. Polish keeper Jan Tomaszewski that night produced one of the most inspired goalkeeping displays ever seen at the stadium. As the man famously branded a clown by Brian Clough before the game, he proved to be anything but.

The result meant that in the space of seven years, England had gone from being world champions to not even qualifying for the finals. Although it was not to happen for six months, failing to qualify for the World Cup gave the FA the reason it had been waiting for to end the managerial reign of Sir Alf Ramsey. A few weeks later on 14th November it was Bobby Moore's 107th and final England appearance. Appropriately enough it was at Wembley, though England went down to Italy by the only goal of the match. It was definitely the end of the golden 1966 era.

Kevin Keegan, who would be as much remembered for his curly perm hairstyle as for his great footballing skills, was the star of the 1974 FA Cup Final. A mighty Liverpool line-up that also featured captain Emlyn Hughes (who would captain England for the first time a week later), Ray Clemence in goal and John Toshack up front, swept Newcastle United aside 3-0. The Magpie's own hero Malcolm Macdonald proving ineffective on this occasion against the Liverpool defence. Keegan provided the first and third goals, and Steve Heighway the second. For pre-match entertainment the crowd were treated to an invitation running of the 3000 metres on the Wembley track. The event was essentially a showcase for the talents of Brendan Foster who agreed to do the event in return for ten tickets to the match for his friends and family. He duly performed and won the race, sporting a black and white striped vest to show his north-east loyalties, and beating Finland's Jula Vaatainen.

The summer of '74 saw a new sport staged as stock car racing held two meetings on the shale track around the pitch. Organised by Trevor Redmond in what was seen as the most spectacular promotion in British Stock Car racing since the sport's 1954 inauguration, the first meeting was held on Saturday 29th June and featured BRISCA F1 Stock

Cars, Hot Rods and various match races, with the pits set up in the bowels of the stadium. The opening race was won by stock car racing legend Stuart Smith in car 391, thereby achieving another 'Wembley First'. Don Evans in car 37 won the F1 race. Sunday 18th August's meeting included BRISCA F2 Stock Car World Championship and the F1 British Stars Trophy. Although it was never going to be a capacity crowd, there were thousands of fans on the terraces who paid an admission fee of 80p. For the more affluent tickets were available in the Royal Box at £2. Both meetings proved that the sport could be held at such a prestigious venue and there was enthusiasm about the excellent presentation and some high quality racing.

With the sport's very nature being one of power, speed and contact between cars, there were many spills and thrills. Several cars clipped the corners of the pitch as they vied for inside position, notably when Gerald Taylor was boxed into a corner and inadvertently span up onto the grass. Worse was to come when Brian Wignall's car spectacularly rolled over and over on the sacred turf. The stock car racing fans and press reflected that with some minor adjustments there was a positive future for the sport at Wembley, *'With more experience, a lessening of the fear of the centre green (i.e. the hallowed turf!) and the knowledge that the two fences, inside and out, will do their job, and any future racing will improve some more'*. However, future racing at Wembley was not to be. Whether for practical reasons or the fear of further damage to the lush Cumberland turf, they were never invited back.

The FA Charity Shield had been held annually since 1908. Originally being a match between a professional and an amateur side, under the stewardship of FA Secretary Ted Croker its profile was raised in 1974 when it was switched to Wembley. It was to be the curtain-raiser to each season with the previous season's League Champions playing the FA Cup winners. The first ended with Liverpool defeating Leeds 6-5 on penalties after a one-all draw. However there was little charity on show. Kevin Keegan and Billy Bremner were both sent off for brawling with each other, with Keegan hurling his shirt onto the Wembley shale in disgust at the decision, and perhaps at his own out-of-character actions. For the next few years if the match was

1974 England v France Schoolboy International (Brent Archive)

drawn the sides kept the shield for six months each. Penalties were later reinstated to ensure a winner. Liverpool held six of the first nine Charity Shields, including the 1977 sharing of the shield with Manchester United after a goalless draw.

The use of Wembley as a venue for major outdoor concerts had been successful in 1972 and such events slowly became standard Wembley fare from then on, with a notable gig occurring on 14th September 1974. This was an all day affair featuring Jesse Colin Young, The Band, Tom Scott and the LA Express, Joni Mitchell and headliners Crosby, Stills, Nash and Young. Amongst the thousands of pioneering music fans was Chris Lewington from Nottingham who still has vivid and happy memories of the day over 30 years on. *'We got to Wembley and had to wait about an hour and a half for the doors to open. We got good seats when we went in. Jesse Colin Young came on at noon and was good, followed by The Band. Then Tom Scott and the LA Express came on at 4.p.m. followed by Joni Mitchell who was brilliant. Crosby, Stills, Nash and Young played from 6.30 right through to 10 p.m. and were excellent. They did 'Ohio' as an encore and the whole place went mad, all 72,000 of us'.* Although everyone had had their doubts

beforehand, *Sounds*, *NME* and *Melody Maker*, the leading music journals of the day all gave a positive report of what was in essence still an early experiment for Wembley.

There was music to the ears for English football that autumn too. After the trauma of missing out on the 1974 World Cup finals, England entered the post-Ramsey era with a new manager, new line up and new team strip. After years of successful club management at Leeds, which included the 1972 FA Cup, Don Revie had taken over from Alf Ramsey. In between Manchester City's Joe Mercer had stepped in as a successful caretaker manager overseeing seven games in five weeks in the summer. The only Wembley match was a one-nil win over Northern Ireland. Revie's first match in charge in October '74 was a 3-0 Wembley win in a European Nations Cup qualifier against Czechoslovakia. This transpired to be no mean feat considering that the Czechs went on to win the competition.

The one hundredth international football match at Wembley was staged on 12th March 1975. England were pitted against their great rivals and World Cup holders West Germany, although on this occasion it was just a friendly. They turned in

Programme of the 1974 International between England and Argentina

one of their best performances for many a year and inspired by Alan Hudson won 2-0, with goals from Colin Bell and Malcolm MacDonald. A month later on 16th April, Malcolm MacDonald scored all five goals in a 5-0 European Nations Cup rout over Cyprus, the most goals ever scored by one player in a Wembley match. A great favourite with the fans, 'Supermac' nevertheless failed to establish himself in the national side and would never play for England at Wembley again, nor score again, earning just a handful more caps. Nevertheless, England's best form of the decade continued with a 5-1 victory over Scotland in May. England's captain during 1975 had been Alan Ball – the last player from the 1966 World Cup winning team still in the England line-up. The Scotland game was to be his last at Wembley and his 72nd and final cap.

The 1975 FA Cup final saw a surprise bonus farewell appearance at Wembley by Bobby Moore. Having finally left his beloved West Ham for Second Division Fulham early in the 1974-75 season, he had already helped his new team-mates put his old ones out of the League Cup at Craven Cottage. In May he was lining up with fellow ex-England stalwart Alan Mullery as the experienced heads against First Division West Ham United. Journalists had their 'Moore Glory' headlines ready, along with incorrectly billing the event as a 'Cockney Cup Final'. Cockneys had little to do with the final headlines with Lancastrian Alan Taylor scoring both goals to go with the pairs he had scored in the quarter and semi-finals. The blonde-haired striker had started the season playing for fourth division Rochdale and ended it a cup winner, in the illustrious company of Trevor Brooking, Billy Bonds and Frank Lampard (Senior). Bobby Moore's glittering Wembley career had ended in a rare defeat, but all things considered, he could probably live with this one. Two years earlier he had said that there *is no place in the world where I get as big a kick out of winning as I do at Wembley. It is the Mecca of football'*.

In that year's Rugby League Challenge Cup Final Ray Dutton and Jim Mills were the heroes for Widnes against arch-rivals Warrington. Centre Mills scored Widnes' only try in a classic final. Ray Dutton kicked five goals and a drop goal in the 14-7 victory. Widnes had led 11-5 at half time the game's turning point came on 50 minutes. A 30 yard drop–goal from Dutton (the first at Wembley under the one point drop-goal rule) was followed by a ten-yard penalty. That widened the gap to seven points, and although 25 minutes remained, Widnes were home and dry.

Three Saturdays later on the last day of May, Wembley was bathed in sunshine when it staged perhaps its most bizarre event. American daredevil stuntman and 1970s icon Evel Knievel hit town. The 36 year old from Butte in Montana, born Robert Craig Knievel, had recently recovered from a near fatal attempt to leap the Snake River Canyon in Idaho on a sky cycle. He managed to keep his nerve for such jumps by having a shot of Wild Turkey whisky beforehand and would have needed this at Wembley. The attempt to jump over thirteen London Transport single-decker buses on his Harley Davidson was considered his most outrageous stunt yet. There was a crowd of over 70,000 at the event and millions more of his fellow Americans watched on the *ABC Wide World of Sports* television programme. After much hype the main event of the afternoon finally arrived when Evel, reportedly on a fee of one million dollars, roared into the stadium. It was a remarkable sight, the like of which had never been seen at Wembley. When the engineers and architects had built the stadium 50 years earlier, they would not have made provision for the 140 feet wooden banking that was erected halfway up the terracing at one end of the ground.

After a series of wheelies and tricks, it was from this steep incline that Evel began his descent, bedecked in a blue jump suit with white and red stars. The buses were lined up side by side between the two penalty areas. Racing down the ramp Evel reached a top speed of 90 miles per hour. He took off twenty feet into the air and amazingly cleared the buses, only to swerve as he hit the landing ramp, and to flip over the handlebars. He skidded over grass and gravel for another forty yards, across the penalty area, eventually ending up on the far end of the stadium. His bike followed him closely behind and hit the prone stuntman hard. A crowd of medics, stadium and security personnel and media raced after him. Despite a stretcher being on hand for him, and with a broken hand, broken pelvis and a compression fracture of a vertebra, he demanded to leave on foot. He asked for the microphone and dramatically announced that the crowd were *'the last people in the world who will ever see me jump. I will never, ever, ever, ever jump again. I am through.'* He left Wembley with tens of thousands chanting his name but didn't keep to his word. Five months later he was back on his bike and back on American television at an amusement park in Ohio. He bettered his Wembley jump and managed to successfully clear 14 Greyhound buses.

Reflecting later on the Wembley jump he said that he *'had an idiot mechanic with me over there. He didn't know his ass from a hole in the ground. He had the gearing on the bike wrong, and it was too late for me to stop and change it. Harley-Davidson couldn't get another gear over there, across the ocean, very fast. I thought I had what I needed when I left, but those buses are awful big in London. So, y'know, I just missed the thing. I couldn't hang on. I never had any suspension on my motorcycle like they have nowadays. But it doesn't matter, you really don't know it till you hit, 'cause you're going so fast, 75 to 85. You can see it comin' when it comes head on at you'.*

> In greyhound racing, three year old Irish dog Westpark Mustard beat the longstanding record of Mick The Miller, with 20 consecutive wins, achieved with trainer Tommy Johnston at Wembley over a period of only 10 months.

The 1976 FA Cup final was the second of the decade to pit Second Division against First. Laurie McMenemy's Southampton took on Tommy Docherty's Manchester United. Although the underdogs, Southampton were on the verge of returning to the upper tier and had a wealth of experience. This included veteran Welsh right back Peter Rodrigues, and England internationals Peter Osgood and Mick Channon. A typically sunny Cup Final day witnessed another Wembley first with Southampton's strip emblazoned with the sponsor's logo. This was a further step along the commercial road from the previously discreet kit manufacturer's logo on the chest, with a line of yellow Admiral logos running down a blue line on Southampton's yellow shirt sleeves. Admiral couldn't lose as they were also sponsor of Manchester United's strip, as well as the England national team. But Manchester United did lose, to a 76th minute goal from Bobby Stokes, who broke into the United half and swept the ball past Alex Stepney.

The first, and to date only, Welsh Wembley victory over England came in a British Championship match in May 1977. An England attack led by Mick Channon failed to score, and the only goal of the game came courtesy of a Leighton James penalty that beat Peter Shilton. The successful Welsh team included future managers Brian Flynn and Terry Yorath (father of present-day presenter Gaby Logan). It wasn't just the Welsh who humiliated their cross-border rivals that year. A few days later Scotland also achieved one of their most famous wins over England. As the teams lined up in front of 100,000 spectators on 4th June it looked like being an even contest. England had an established line up of Ray Clemence in goal, a back four of Phil Neal, Brian Greenhoff (substituted by Trevor Cherry), Dave Watson and Mick Mills; a midfield trio of Emlyn Hughes, Brian Talbot and Ray Kennedy (substituted by Dennis Tueart), and three upfront; Trevor Francis, Mick Channon and Stuart Pearson. Scotland fielded the core of what was to become their 1978 World Cup team: Alan Rough in goal, Danny McGrain, Willie Donachie, Alex Forsyth and Gordon McQueen at the back; Bruce Rioch, Don Masson (substituted by Archie Gemmill), Asa Hartford and Willie Johnson in midfield, and the powerful combination up front of Kenny Dalglish and Joe Jordan (substituted by Lou Macari).

After goals from McQueen and Dalglish had secured a 2-1 victory for the Scots, there was a celebratory pitch invasion by thousands, with fans tearing up seats, part of the turf, dancing in the goalmouths and jumping on the crossbars, causing one to collapse under the weight. This jubilation cost an estimated £15,000 in repairs. Future Scottish star, and now manager, Gordon Strachan, was in the crowd for his first trip to Wembley. *'It felt like we were the only people left in the stands and eventually we were asked by a policeman if we wanted to come onto the pitch. So I trod on the famous turf at Wembley for the first time at the*

Programme of the 1977 Home International between England and Wales

After Don Revie's defection to the United Arab Emirates. 55 year old Ron Greenwood was coaxed out of retirement to take over the managerial reigns midway through a World Cup qualification campaign. 16th November 1977 saw the crucial qualifying group decider between England and Italy. A crowd of 92,500 cheered England to a 2-0 win with a Kevin Keegan header and Trevor Brooking shot beating Italian goalie Dino Zoff. New caps Bob Latchford and Steve Coppell played well and England also successfully employed two wingers in the form of Coppell on the right and Peter Barnes on the left. Frustratingly the win was to no avail as it was Dino Zoff's Italy who were Argentina-bound for the 1978 World Cup Finals on goal difference.

The Netherlands also visited in 1977 and inspired by Johan Cruyff they showed England just how far away the hosts were from a place at the top of the international hierarchy. A team that included Ruud Krol, Johan Neeskins, Johnny Rep and Willy van der Kerhof secured a 2-0 win with both goals scored by Jan Peters. An England team seemingly containing a wealth of talent in Clemence, Keegan, Brooking and Beattie still had no answers. The Netherlands were warming up for the 1978 World Cup Finals, where they were to be losing finalists. Kevin Keegan was amongst those who wondered if the under-performing of England in the 1970s was partially the fault of the stadium itself. *'Wembley so resembles a foreign ground, with a wide track separating the pitch from the crowd, that visitors often feel more at home than our own players.'* Football authority and journalist Jack Rollin also wrote that Wembley had a strange influence on visiting countries which was at one extreme awe-inspiring to them, yet also made them more determined to lift their performance.

Domestically the 1977 League Cup Final produced the first Wembley final to end in a goalless draw. Aston Villa and Everton battled on at Hillsborough

TREVOR REDMOND'S

AUTO SPEED CIRCUITS

presents

FOR THE FIRST TIME EVER AT

Wembley

£500 1974 WEMBLEY STOCK CAR CHAMPIONSHIP

Plus Internationally Famous Drivers from the World of Motor Racing

WHO WILL WIN THE £100 RECORD ATTEMPT ?
ROGER CLARKE — Rally ?   STUART SMITH — Stocks ?
BARRY LEE — Hot Rod ?
TOM PITCHER — F.2 ?   DAVE CHISHOLM — F.1 ?
or the world famous grand prix drivers ?

Choice of their own car or Shell Sport Mexicos

Also the racing D.J. NOEL EDMONDS and other stars

Sponsors: Car & Car Conversions — Custom Car & B.P.

Saturday 29th June at 7.15

Come early — Book now · · Wembley Box Office 01-902-1234

Seats under cover £1, £1.50; Royal Box Area £2

Children under 14 half-price   Special prices for parties of 20 or more

Turnstile admissions available on day

LUCKY SOUVENIR PROGRAMME

Stock Car racing at Wembley (both photographs © Dave Carter)

'*Wembley!*' The name was magic no matter what sport was taking part under the famous Twin Towers. My sport was speedway and my first impression of the old Empire Stadium was from when I and a couple of schoolfriends came down from Glasgow on the overnight bus to watch the World Speedway Final. A very long journey in those pre-Motorway days, but well worth it for the glitz and glamour of a Wembley World Final. It certainly was glitzy as at that time 90,000 fans packed the grandstands and when the race started, all the stadium lights went out except for the ribbon of floodlights around the track. The bikes were all chrome-plated British JAP engined machines which sparkled under the floodlights, and with the riders all wearing highly-polished black leathers, it looked more like a scene from Ben Hur than a motorcycle race meeting.

Although I lived in Glasgow, Wembley played a big part in my early life. As a young lad riding Cycle Speedway, our team, the Mansewood Lions, wore body colours which had been donated by the Wembley team and, although I didn't know it at the time, many years later, I was to ride for, and captain, the REAL Wembley Lions when they returned to speedway in 1970 and 1971. I had been riding for the Edinburgh Monarchs and was in Australia when Wembley reopened (for speedway). I was told that most of the Edinburgh team had been transferred to London to form the new Wembley Lions and they were laying a new track outside of the football pitch and the Lions would be back in the First Division. The team manager would be former Wembley Lion and double World Champion, Freddie Williams, with another former World Champion, Sweden's Ove Fundin as our top star, so things were looking good. Life was exciting for a young Scot in the bright lights of London!

Being part of Wembley Speedway was a huge boost for my career and the magic of the stadium attracted many outside sponsors who wanted to be part of the action. As a rider, the track was quite difficult to ride, but you got great satisfacton when you got it right and won your races. Although our League matches didn't attract the huge crowds of a World Final, the Wembley fans always created a great atmosphere and, after the meeting, could meet the riders in The Long Bar in the stadium. Top BBC DJ's of the time, Ed Stewart and David Hamilton, were the track announcers every Saturday and even bravely rode our 500cc fire-breathing speedway bikes in a special celebrity race one night although Ed, at almost six foot tall, had a lot of trouble fitting into my smaller tartan race leathers.

The loss of Wembley Stadium to speedway was a great blow to the sport, but sharing the Stadium with football was not ideal as the corners of the football pitch had to be removed to make way for the speedway turns. So by 1972, the Lions had to close and in the new Wembley there is no place for speedway. But no matter what your sport was, if you competed at Wembley, that memory will stay with you forever and we will all miss the twin towers.

Bert Harkins, former Wembley Lions Speedway Captain

Bert Harkins in action at Wembley (© Bert Harkins)

and Old Trafford before the Midlanders finally won a thrilling second replay. Aston Villa striker and now TV pundit, Andy Gray blamed Wembley for not winning the trophy at the first attempt. *'Too many of us seemed a little overcome by the occasion. Few of us had had experience of Wembley or Cup Finals and this showed in our play. It was our worst display of the season and I felt very sorry for our fans. My lasting memory of the final is the empty feeling I had, when, at the end of the game, we went up the steps to the Royal Box, and came straight down again.'* 1977 also saw only the second entry on the 'Footballers Sent Off in Full Wembley Internationals' table with Gilbert Dresch of Luxembourg joining Argentina's Rattin, after being dismissed in their 5-0 World Cup Qualifier defeat.

10th May 1978 saw Liverpool become the first British club to lift the European Cup for the second time, with a 1-0 win over Belgian side Bruges, in Wembley's fourth hosting of the event. Although on the whole it was a game that didn't live up to its billing, Kenny Dalglish rounded off his first season for the Anfield club in style, scoring the only goal of the game with a delicate chip from the right side of the penalty area after 65 minutes. Also in the Liverpool line-up that night before the 92,000 crowd, was defender Alan Hansen, now a fixture as a pundit in the BBC's football coverage.

Leeds won successive Rugby League Challenge Cup Finals in the late seventies, bringing their Wembley total to five successes from eight final appearances. In 1977 they saw off Widnes 16-7, and narrowly defeated St. Helens 14-12 the following year. With a try, three goals and a drop goal, the 1977 game was to be an unbelievable Challenge Cup debut for

Leeds scrum half Kevin Dick, finding himself playing alongside prop forward, Steve Pitchford – nicknamed 'the bionic barrel' for his solid build and tough approach.

History was made in November 1978 when Nottingham Forest right back Viv Anderson became the first black player to represent England at Wembley, in a win against Czechoslovakia. But the decade had mostly been an age of lost opportunities for the England squad. The 1970s had seen a crop of flair footballers breaking through into the English team to grace the stadium, gradually replacing the old guard of the 1966 and Mexico 1970 World Cup campaigns. But despite flamboyant players such as Peter Barnes, Stan Bowles, Tony Currie, Alan Hudson, Rodney Marsh, Dave Thomas and Frank Worthington all earning caps, England had. a dismal qualification record for the major tournaments. Defeated at home by West Germany in the European Championships quarter final in 1972, they also failed to qualify for the 1974 and 1978 World Cups and the 1976 European Championship, (which took on a new format of the final eight playing in one country).

A last minute winner from Sunderland was the dramatic climax of the 1979 Cup Final; Alan Sunderland of Arsenal in this case however, and not a return visit for the Black Cats. Being the fourth cup final of the decade for Arsenal and the third for Manchester United, this should have been a classic but it only really came alive at the end of a game that was otherwise very forgettable. Arsenal took an early lead through Brian Talbot, with Frank Stapleton making it 2-0 before half-time. With 85 minutes gone the game seemed over, until United somehow pulled back two quick goals through Sammy McIlroy and Gordon McQueen. With United still celebrating Liam Brady raced up to the other end to cross for Alan Sunderland to snatch a last gasp winner, breaking red Mancunian hearts but to the great relief of his team-mates who moments earlier thought they had thrown it all away.

The 1980s were a time of cultural and political change, and this was reflected in the usage of Wembley Stadium. While hundreds of thousands of protesters marched on the streets of London against nuclear weapons and apartheid, hundreds of thousands of sports fans continued to march down Olympic Way for long-established prestigious Wembley fixtures. Similarly, the stadium's huge capacity ensured it was firmly established as a premier venue for many of the biggest rock and pop acts in the world. Politics and religion also found their way to Wembley. Although Live Aid in 1985 was a music festival, it was of course underpinned by the public and pop world's growing awareness of global inequalities. Continuing in the campaigning vein, the 1988 Wembley concert for the still-imprisoned Nelson Mandela gave further impetus to change in South Africa. The stadium was also packed out for the Papal Mass of 1982 and a visit from American evangelist preacher Billy Graham in 1989.

For Saturday 3rd May the city of Hull was a ghost town, as fans of both Hull and Hull Kingston Rovers journeyed to Wembley for the 1980 Rugby League Challenge Cup Final, boosting the Wembley crowd to 95,000. Humbersiders who hadn't made the trip to London settled down to watch BBC coverage. Hull Kingston Rover's star player was Roger Millward who had probably his most memorable match. Hailed as possibly the best ever player for Great Britain, let alone Hull Kingston Rovers, he also went onto become a successful coach. But in May 1980 'Roger the Dodger', as TV commentator Eddie Waring had christened him, was the player-coach as The Robins beat neighbours Hull 10-5. An eighth minute try from man of the match Steve Hubbard set them on the way. He also later scored three goals. After fifteen minutes Millward was involved in an incident with Hull hooker Ron Wileman, resulting in him receiving a broken jaw. Unbelievably he managed to continue playing for the full 80 minutes and scored a drop kick into the bargain. In what turned out to be his last match,

the courageous captain climbed the 39 steps of the Royal Box and received the trophy from the Queen Mother. Of his broken jaw Millward said, *'The bone was out of place and I could feel it wasn't right. Fortunately, a few seconds later, I went in to tackle Hull's Steve Norton and my jaw caught his knee. The impact caused my jaw to click back in place and I was able to carry on playing.'* As coach he took the Rovers back to Wembley the following year only to lose to Widnes, and again in 1986, only to be defeated once again narrowly by Castleford.

A week later, Arsenal started the 1980s where they had left off in the 1970s, namely with another FA Cup Final appearance. In what was only the third all-London Cup Final, as holders, Arsenal were confident of overcoming Second Division West Ham United. However, a rare, low header from Trevor Brooking in the thirteenth minute beat Pat Jennings in the Arsenal goal, and proved to be the only goal of the game. The Hammers came close to doubling their lead late in the second half, when Paul Allen broke through only to be unceremoniously hauled down by Scottish International Willie Young. Although denied a goal, Allen still had cause to celebrate with a winner's medal and the honour of becoming the youngest ever player to appear in a Cup Final, aged 17 years and 256 days.

It was the centenary FA Cup Final in 1981, a prolonged epic between Manchester City and Tottenham Hotspur. Spurs paraded the first two Argentinians to partake in a Cup Final, whom they had imported after they helped Argentina to win the 1978 World Cup. These were the two midfielders, the bearded Ricardo 'Ricky' Villa and the diminutive Osvaldo 'Ossie' Ardiles. The first match was a disappointment for Villa as he was substituted but his moments of glory were to come in the replay. In the first match City's Tommy Hutchinson scored both goals; a spectacular flying header on the half-hour, and an own goal when a Glenn Hoddle free kick deflected off his shoulder and past England's third choice goalkeeper Joe Corrigan. It

Programme of the 1982 European Championship match between England and Luxembourg

was quite an afternoon for Hutchinson, at 33 years old, the oldest player on the pitch.

So the first FA Cup Final replay ever held at Wembley took place the following Thursday. Sandwiched between the finals was an England versus Brazil friendly which the visitors won 1-0 through Zico. The replay was worth the extra day's wait, producing a long-remembered match. Ricky Villa put the Londoners ahead on eight minutes but within three minutes Steve Mackenzie had volleyed a fantastic equaliser. BBC commentator John Motson was not alone in believing that it would have been remembered as one of the greatest ever Cup Final goals, had it not been surpassed by the winning goal in the same match. Early in the second half referee Keith Hackett awarded what was only the fifth ever FA Cup Final penalty at the stadium. City's Kevin Reeves shot home to give then a 2-1 lead. Tottenham applied pressure and Garth Crooks levelled the scores after 60 minutes. The stage was set for a winning goal that was one of the best ever seen at Wembley. Ricky Villa weaved his way infield from close to the left touchline, around an array of light blue defenders in the penalty area, before slotting home the winner. Under the floodlights, which added wonderfully to the atmosphere, Spurs captain Steve Perryman collected the trophy.

Despite Wembley now comfortably catering for both music and football in its event repertoire, the combining of the two in the shape of teams' FA Cup songs in this era was derided by all but the most devoted fan. Cockney pop duo Chas and Dave's single 'Ossie's on His Way to Wembley, (Tottenham's gonna do it again)', complete with the Argentinian's accented rhyming line 'in the cup for Totting-ham' reached a new nadir in the annals of appalling pop and football combos. Tottenham repeated their footballing feat (thankfully not the musical one) a year later, beating Queens Park Rangers 1-0 in a replay by a penalty. That Tottenham team were well equipped for the rigours of knockout football, and reached the 1982 League Cup final as well, only to lose narrowly to Liverpool.

A late summer evening in 1981 witnessed the last ever speedway event at Wembley with the holding of that year's World Individual Championship Final. The sport left the stadium in style as after winning four heats, Bruce Penhall still had to give it all he had in an exciting final race. The 21 year old Californian passed former World Champion Ole Olsen on the last bend to secure the trophy. Olsen was runner-up and third place went to Tommy Knudsen. After over 50 years of club and international speedway, these were the final laps of the cinder track for a sport which, in its heyday had helped secure financial stability and a future for Wembley in its uncertain early years. Bruce Penhall retired from speedway the following year, moving on to an acting career which included a regular role in the TV series 'Chips'.

England under Ron Greenwood managed to qualify for the 1982 World Cup in Spain. This was the first successful qualification campaign since 1962, having gained automatic qualification in 1966 as hosts, and for Mexico 1970 as holders. Being England they did this the hard way of course, succumbing to defeats in their away matches with Norway, Romania and Switzerland and dropping points with a 0-0 home Wembley draw with Romania. In November 1981 they were left needing a win over Hungary at Wembley to secure passage to the finals as group runners-up. The nation waited with baited breath. Would it be Poland 1973 all over again? Such was the importance of the game, that the Football League agreed to suspend all First Division fixtures the weekend before the match, which was the first time this had been done since 1946. 92,000 crammed into Wembley, millions more bit their fingernails in front of televisions across England, and a collective sigh of relief was heard as Paul Mariner of Ipswich Town slotted home the only goal of the game.

Warming up for Spain, the Home International against Northern Ireland in February 1982 was a resounding win for England. They scored four times without reply, the quartet of goal scorers being Bryan Robson, Ray Wilkins, Glenn Hoddle and captain Kevin Keegan, making his last Wembley appearance for England. The most notable event of a winter's night was the opening goal by Bryan Robson after just 44 seconds, the fastest ever scored in a Wembley international.

1982 was also the year that the great stadium witnessed a number of events that it had never seen the like of before. Most notable of all was the first ever visit of a pontiff to Britain. Nearly a decade after an inspired display at Wembley from Polish goalkeeper, Jan Tomaszewski, another Polish goalkeeper was in action at the stadium. Trying to save souls rather than goals, Pope John Paul II had a busy day on 29th May. A year after surviving an assassination attempt, he had a morning meeting in Canterbury Cathedral with Archbishop Basil Hulme, itself a historical breakthrough. Courtesy of the white vehicle dubbed the Popemobile he paraded round Wembley. There were 2,500 priests amongst the 80,000 strong crowd and the Pope said mass from an altar erected on the pitch. Pope John Paul II was a useful goalkeeper in his youth, and throughout his life was a keen football fan who followed the fortunes of many teams, including Barcelona, Fulham, and Liverpool. However, his local team Krakovia Krakow were the team he actually supported. His Wembley words of *'peace be with you'* had added poignancy, coming as they did with the Falklands War raging in the South Atlantic at the time, and Britain's inner cities still smouldering with tension after the previous summer's riots.

The Pope wasn't the only big name to sell out Wembley that summer. Simon and Garfunkel were touring again after a break of ten years. Following a successful reunion concert in New York's Central Park the previous year, they performed to a Wembley packed to its 72,000 concert capacity on 19th June. The duo, now over 40 but still in their prime, ran flawlessly through tracks such as 'Sounds of Silence', 'America' and 'Homeward Bound'. The other big name band to pack out Wembley that June, was the Rolling Stones. As part of their 'Tattoo You' World Tour, they performed for two nights on 25th and 26th June, supported by Black Uhuru and the J Geils Band. Still going strong after twenty years, and even enjoying a new lease of life with the boom in stadium rock, Mick Jagger, Keith Richards, Charlie Watts, Ron Wood and Bill Wyman delivered a set of crowd pleasers. The infrastructure behind them enabled a world arena tour complete with huge stage with hydraulic platform, video screens and a set of avant-garde art. By the time that Wembley closed in 2000, The Stones had played and filled the stadium an incredible twelve times. But in typically casual manner, when asked in '82 how he would approach the challenge of first playing at Britain's premier venue, Keith

Richards replied *'from Heathrow'*.

Although the vast majority of patrons obtained tickets legitimately for Wembley concerts, there were often stories of 'enterprising' folk who tried to bribe their way in. This was the case at most large scale concerts, and inevitably a handful managed to get through the turnstiles that way. Rolling Stones or Simon and Garfunkel concerts cost about £20 for a face value ticket, but a surreptitiously placed fiver might get you into the ground, or then again get you into serious trouble. This practice will become a thing of the past in the Wembley with the advance in 21st century ticketing methods and entrances to the stadium.

After a spirited World Cup campaign in Spain, where England didn't lose a match but were nevertheless knocked out in the second round group phase, Ron Greenwood stepped down as manager to be replaced by Bobby Robson. Just like Alf Ramsey, Robson came from a successful spell as Ipswich Town manager, and also just like Ramsey, he went on to receive a knighthood. When he had won the 1978 FA Cup against Arsenal, Robson said of Wembley's most prestigious event, *'The FA Cup Final is the greatest single match outside the World Cup Final – and it's ours.'* He now had an opportunity to try and capture the World Cup as well. He could not have dreamt of a better start to his England role. His first match in charge at Wembley was on 15th December 1982, in a Euro '84 Group Three Qualifying match against Luxembourg. Christmas certainly came early to Wembley that December night as England recorded their biggest ever margin of victory at Wembley. They scored nine goals without reply against Luis Pilot's hapless Luxembourgoise. The tiny crowd (by Wembley international standards) of 33,980 that had put Christmas shopping and parties to one side and braved a trip out to Wembley were amply rewarded. There were four first half goals, commencing with an own goal after 18 minutes. Steve Coppell and Tony Woodcock added two more, before Luther Blisset became the first black goal scorer for England, just before half time. The Watford striker added his second in the second half, and nine minutes later Stoke City's winger Mark Chamberlain became the second black player to score for England. There were three more goals in the last

THIS PROGRAMME SAVES LIVES

PRICE £5

Programme of the 1985 Live Aid Concert (Brent Archive)

Live Aid mural, Olympic Way

five minutes, as Blissett completed a hat-trick, Glenn Hoddle made his mark, and even Liverpool right back Phil Neal got in on the act. Icelandic referee Hreidar Jonsson blew the final whistle with England looking to break into double figures.

Brighton and Hove Albion were enjoying a rare spell in the top flight in 1982-83, and after a good cup run their loyal fans were in disbelief to also find themselves in the 1983 FA Cup Final. However, it was no fluke that they had reached the final. Although doomed to relegation back to Division Two that season, they had claimed some major scalps on the road to Wembley, knocking out the likes of Newcastle United, Manchester City and Liverpool en route. Inevitably they were touted as the underdogs, and rightly so considering they were up against Manchester United. United were out to make up for their last visit to the stadium when they had lost the 1979 final, but Jimmy Melia's spirited Brighton team made a decent match of it. The final was close and exciting, going into extra time after Gordon Smith and Gary Stevens had scored for Brighton, with Ray Wilkins and Frank Stapleton scoring for Manchester United. In the last minute of extra time Brighton's Gordon Smith was clear through on goal with just Gary Bailey to beat in the United goal. Time seemed to stand still, everyone watching echoing the radio commentator Peter Jones' scream of *'and Smith must score…'*. Unfortunately for Albion he didn't but the phrase entered football parlance. Brighton fans had a good sense of humour and

with the advent of the self-publishing fanzine era from the mid 1980s, a Brighton fanzine was produced, entitled *'And Smith Must Score'*. So, for the third successive year the FA Cup Final required a replay. But the chance for a famous Seagulls' victory had flown. The true gulf between the two teams was in evidence in the replay, which yielded four goals, this time all for Manchester United.

Surprisingly, despite their frequent appearances beneath the Twin Towers, Mersey rivals Everton and Liverpool had never played against each other there. This changed in 1984 and by the end of the decade they had met there five times: in a League Cup Final, two Charity Shields and two FA Cup Finals. The first Wembley Mersey derby was the League Cup Final of 1984. It was a close affair in awful weather that produced no goals, just the controversy of a spurned Everton penalty appeal when Alan Hansen handballed. The replay was held nearer to home at Maine Road Manchester, and Liverpool scored the only goal of the game. This was Liverpool's fourth successive League Cup final victory and, as losers, Everton were in good company. West Ham United, Tottenham Hotspur and Manchester United were all famous names in the Wembley story that had been beaten in the early eighties by the rampant and irresistible Reds.

April 1984 saw the last Home International Championship match to be played at Wembley – a 1-0 win for England over Northern Ireland before a crowd of just 24,000. With the demands of international football now being so much greater than when this competition was devised, it increasingly felt like a competition too many. On top of this, the increasing security problems of fixtures in Northern Ireland, due to 'the troubles', made sides reluctant to travel there, and so the competition was scrapped. The most popular fixture, the annual England-Scotland encounter, was however revived from '86 to '89 as part of the Rous Cup – essentially a set of friendlies involving England and Scotland and an invited third nation.

Elton John visited Wembley twice in 1984 and experienced mixed emotions. His beloved Watford, who under Graham Taylor had rapidly risen from Fourth to First Division and European football, reached their first FA Cup Final. Everton were their opponents, and made up for their League Cup Final defeat in the March by winning 2-0. Goals from Graeme Sharp and Andy Gray detracted from a plucky Watford team that included John Barnes. The second goal was controversial with Gray seeming to head the ball out of The Hornets' keeper Steve Sherwood's hand, but the goal was allowed. Elton was back at the end of June, where he headlining the 'Summer of '84' Concert. Other acts were Paul Young, Kool And The Gang, Nik Kershaw and Wang Chung. Elton, resplendent in straw boater and black bow tie, performed a lively set with a mix of new and old standards. 'Philadelphia Freedom', 'Rocket Man', 'Daniel', 'I'm Still Standing' and 'I Guess That's Why They Call it the Blues' were included, the latter perhaps sung to Everton FC.

The first major football final of 1985 was decided by a deflected goal from veteran Scots midfielder Asa Hartford. This helped Norwich City to their first ever Wembley trophy; the Milk (League) Cup, against Sunderland. Nine years previously Hartford had helped Manchester City overcome Newcastle United in the League Cup final, thanks to a Dennis Tueart overhead kick. That season's FA Cup Final between Everton and Manchester United was also a tight affair. It entered extra time goalless and with United down to ten men after centre half Kevin Moran had become the first player to be sent off in an FA Cup Final. Then Norman Whiteside ran down the right wing and curled a twenty-yard shot past Welsh goalkeeper Neville Southall for the goal of the season to win the Cup for United.

Widnes took the Rugby League Challenge Cup for the seventh time at Wembley in the May '84 final where they beat Wigan 19-6. At the time this was the most ever wins at Wembley, although it would be their opposition that day would later surpass this achievement. But setting the hallowed turf on fire in '84 was 20 year old Joe Lydon, who once in each half ran the length of the pitch to score incredible tries. Wigan returned in '85 to take the trophy themselves beating Hull 28-24 in possibly the best final of the decade. Although his stay in English Rugby was to last only six months, Wigan's Australian Test star Brett Kenny made the most of his one Challenge Cup Final opportunity. Integral in the three tries scored by his team-mates he also got on the scoresheet himself with a wonderful solo effort.

13th July 1985 was a day that some of the well meaning minds of the music industry again tried to change the murky world of international politics. Bob Geldof and Midge Ure were the main brains behind the biggest gig ever seen – Live Aid.

Pope John Paul II at Wembley
(© Arundel & Brighton Walking Pilgrimages)

Working at the stadium may have seemed a good way to get access to a wide range of mouth-watering events but it wasn't necessarily the case. There was a lot of part-time work, including staffing the bars, but that involved serving endless pints of expensive frothy beer in plastic pots to grouchy fans who had waited an age to get served. There were little thanks and even less chance to nip out to catch a few minutes of a match or gig. The rate of pay was good for the time though, with a barman for an event earning about £20 in 1982. There were high pressure jobs as well, particularly in an age when stadium disasters were becoming horribly too common. Ted Pascoe was a Fire Prevention Officer at Wembley Stadium and the Arena, and involved in all the major national sports and show events assessing the fire risks. He met many stars including Mick Jagger and Simon & Garfunkel and was involved in the FA Cup Finals. He recalls, 'It wasn't all roses. The stadium was a place to see when it was filled to the roof-tops with fans for a pop concert. They used to lay a tarpaulin on the pitch and people would cram close to the stage. Getting people out of there in an emergency would have been a nightmare, it was lucky nothing serious happened'.

Around 1.5 billion people are believed to have watched around the world in 170 countries, on television and at the events themselves. As well as the main concert at Wembley, there were Live Aid events in countries as geopolitically diverse as the USA, the USSR, Australia, Japan, Norway and Yugoslavia. Carrying on from the success of the Band-Aid single, which had raised millions for famine-stricken Ethiopia when Western governments were loathe to act, Live Aid raised an estimated £150 million. It also raised the consciousness of many of the public who were hitherto indifferent to, or ignorant of, the issues of justice in the Developing World.

The Wembley event showcased many of the most popular acts of the day in the world of British pop. A number of popular BBC Radio One Disc Jockeys introduced the acts, namely Richard Skinner, Andy Peebles, Tommy Vance and Noel Edmonds. Promoter Harvey Goldsmith, actor John Hurt and comedians Billy Connolly, Mel Smith and Griff Rhys Jones also threw their weight behind the cause. After a Royal Seal of approval from the Prince and Princess of Wales, the reason the vast majority of the 72,000 crowd were there got underway; the music. Lest the crowd forget the real purpose the event was being staged – the famine in Ethiopia – the seriousness of the message was underlined continually throughout the day, on stage and throughout the various parallel Live Aid events around the world and infamously by Bob Geldof during live TV coverage.

The acts at Wembley, most of whom performed three or four of their best known tracks, were: Status Quo, The Style Council, The Boomtown Rats, Adam Ant, Ultravox, Spandau Ballet, Elvis Costello, Nik Kershaw, Sade, Sting, Howard Jones, Bryan Ferry, Paul Young and Alison Moyet, U2, Dire Straits, Queen, David Bowie, The Who, Elton John, Kiki Dee and Wham and Paul McCartney. Dire Straits were probably the biggest band of the time, and they performed 'Money For Nothing' and 'Sultans of Swing'. U2 and Queen were the other bands of megastar status who performed, both of whom were to sell out Wembley Stadium on their own over the next two summers. The front man of Queen, Freddie Mercury, put on perhaps one of the best performances of his life. Described as the consummate showman he had the crowd in the palm of his hand. Phil Collins, the Genesis drummer and vocalist who had branched out into a successful solo career, managed the feat of playing at Wembley and later at the Philadelphia Live Aid concert in the same day, assisted by several hours time difference between the events and the use of Concorde. Appropriately his set at both events included 'In the Air Tonight' and 'Against All Odds'.

As organisers of the event, it was no real surprise to see Geldof's own band, The Boomtown Rats and Midge Ure's Ultravox elevated for the occa-

Tickets from events at Wembley and at Wembley Arena

sion. Most of the pop acts at Live Aid were at their peak and their stars were soon to wane. Exceptions who were to be found still alive and singing well into the 21st century were solo artists Bowie, McCartney, Sting, Elton John and Paul Weller. Weller's Style Council were probably about the coolest band on view at Wembley, their track 'Internationalists' summing up the spirit of the day. The grand finale of the event had all the bands and artists coming back onto the stage together to perform the Band-Aid fundraising single, 'Do They Know It's Christmas'.

Despite football clubs continually complaining about fixture pile-ups, two more competitions were initiated in the 1985-86 season; The Full Members Cup (for clubs in the top two divisions)

and The Freight Rover Trophy (for the lower two divisions and top non-league clubs). To those fans and teams not involved in the finals, the competitions were derided as meaningless, but to the eventual winners they were a welcome boost. Winners of the inaugural competitions in 1986 at Wembley were Chelsea and Bristol Rovers who both had barren trophy cabinets and for their fans any trophy was better than none.

The more prestigious League Cup (even though there was no UEFA Cup place due to a European ban on English clubs after the 1985 Heysel tragedy) was still sought after. On 20th April 1986 90,300 fans watched manager Jim Smith's old club confront his new one, as Oxford United took on Queens Park Rangers – both then First Division

Players' changing room and baths – late 1980s (© Andy Davidson)

sides. Oxford took a shock lead near half-time as Trevor Hebberd scored from a John Aldridge pass. They then managed to keep QPR at bay in the second half, iincreasing their lead when Ray Houghton scored. Late in the game a John Aldridge shot was saved but Jeremy Charles followed up for an emphatic 3-0 win and a massive day for the Oxford fans. It was the largest winning margin of a Wembley League Cup Final at the time. In a gracious gesture, Oxford manager Maurice Evans insisted that the club's long serving physiotherapist, 72 year old Ken Fish, should collect a medal instead of himself.

In May 1986 the first Merseyside derby FA Cup Final ended with Liverpool winning 3-1 over their rivals from across Stanley Park. Everton's Gary Lineker put the Blues ahead in the first half, but his opposite number, Welsh international Ian Rush, equalised. Australian Craig Johnston put the Reds in front and Ian Rush grabbed his second in the closing minutes. Lineker lost on the day but had a brighter summer ahead of him, ending as the top goal scorer in the Mexico World Cup finals. The Liverpool line up that day included Alan Hansen and Mark Lawrenson who would become regular sparring partners for Lineker on BBC's *'Match of the Day'*.

Boxer Frank Bruno was a favourite son of Britain, eventually as much at home in pantomimes as in the boxing ring, but his first world title fight was on 19th July 1986. 'Terrible' Tim Witherspoon from Philadelphia was his opponent at Wembley Stadium for the World Heavyweight Challenge Bout. Henry Cooper and Mohammed Ali (formerly Cassius Clay), who had fought at Wembley 23 years earlier, met again in the ring before the Bruno bout. Ali jokingly went to take off his jacket, and Cooper pointed to his scarred eyebrows, a legacy from that previous fight. Bruno and Witherspoon went through ten rounds without much incident, but the eleventh produced drama. Both men took right hand blows to the head, but Witherspoon got Frank in a corner after a decisive blow to his chin. He pummeled at the flailing Bruno and referee Isidro Rodriguez had to intervene. There had been no British World Heavyweight champion for over a hundred years, and it wasn't going to change that night, though Frank's dream was eventually fulfilled nine years later.

The next month, on 3rd August 1986, American Football debuted at Wembley. 82,000 watched as the Chicago Bears defeated the Dallas Cowboys 17-6, in The American Bowl (a series of pre-season matches held outside the USA). It was the start of an annual pilgrimage of the American game to Wembley. 1987 saw the LA Rams narrowly beat the Denver Broncos 28-27; 1988 was a 27-21 win for the Miami Dolphins over San Francisco 49ers; and in August 1989 Philadelphia Eagles overcame Cleveland Browns 17-13.

Queen played Wembley in the summer as part of their 26 date UK and European 'Magic' tour. Acknowledged to be their finest performance, it also turned out to be one of their last. Guitarist Brian May reflected, *'The Wembley concerts in 1986 were the pinnacle for us. We were at our height band-wise, and Freddie [Mercury] developed this phenomenal way of dealing with stadium audiences. Being back home in London playing two sell-out nights was such a big, big occasion for us. None us realised that this would be almost the last time we played together.'*

The greyhound world in the 1980s belonged to Ballyregan Bob, who set a new record of 32 straight wins in 1985 and 1986. His best race at Wembley came in the semi final of the St. Leger. Two other dogs in the race fell yet somehow Ballyregan Bob managed to hurdle over them and catch up with race leader, Evening Light (who happened to be his brother), who had been several lengths ahead. With his trademark burst of speed on the home run he achieved a famous victory.

Coventry City reached their first ever FA Cup Final in 1987. For a team that had spent decades in the top flight it was a long time coming. Up against seasoned cup specialists Tottenham, they were going to have their work cut out. It was one of the most open and exhilarating finals for many a year. It was 2-1 to Tottenham when Coventry's Keith Houchen and Cyrille Regis broke, and the ball was fed out to David Bennett on the right wing who whipped in a

cross. Houchen launched himself speculatively and spectacularly to equalise with a low diving header. The match went into extra time where it was decided in the cruellest of manners, with Tottenham's Gary Mabbutt scoring an own goal. The cup was bound for Highfield Road for the first time.

Two major British acts played the stadium in the summer of 1987. Both had started out in the sixties with cult followings, and were elevated throughout the seventies to the height of international rock stardom. Popular in Europe, Asia, Australasia and with the North American arena market conquered too, it was just a matter of time before David Bowie and Genesis performed in their home capital. After three days of rehearsal at the stadium, Bowie's 'Glass Spider' tour, which lasted 86 performances in fifteen countries, played to a Wembley audience. Recent hits such as 'Absolute Beginners' and 'China Girl' were heard along with older classics such as 'Sons of the Silent Age', 'Heroes' and 'Fame'. Then for the first four days of July it was Genesis and their 'Invisible Touch' tour that filled the stadium. Now as just the trio of Tony Banks, Phil Collins and Mike Rutherford, they were joined on stage by Americans Daryl Stuermer (guitar) and Chester Thompson (drums), and became the first band to sell out four Wembley Stadium

American Football comes to Wembley (© Andy Davidson)

Wealdstone and Boston United prepare for the 1985 FA Trophy Final

shows. As usual their stage act was enhanced by cutting edge technology, Genesis being the first band to use Vari Lites, Jumbotron screens and the Prism sound system, all of which are now standard features of arena rock concerts. Their set repertoire included a mix of their biggest '80s and favourite album tracks such as 'Mama', 'Abacab', and 'Home by the Sea'. The lighting show was well suited to an arena such as Wembley, with the purple back-lights shining into the north-west London night, exploding into flame colours, twinkling into whites, then sheets of blue and green, as the band, complete with drum duo, launched into the fans' favourite set closer 'Los Endos' with gusto.

There were some improvements to the fast fading stadium in 1988, most notably an upgrade to electronic scoreboards in 1988. They measured 82 feet (25m) wide by 15 feet (4.5m) high with 20 feet (6m) advertising panels. They were first tried out in the England v. Brazil Schools International Match in March, which the English boys won 2-0.

The 1988 League Cup produced an unlikely winner in Luton Town, enjoying a rare spell in Division One at the time. It was the Bedfordshire club's first trip down the M1 to Wembley for a final since their 1959 FA Cup defeat. Wembley regulars Arsenal were their opponents and they were heading for another trophy with a 2-1 lead late into the game. Ten minutes remained when Arsenal were awarded a penalty, and it seemed that the cup was surely theirs. But Luton goalkeeper Andy Dibble managed to save, and Luton were inspired. Danny Wilson scrambled home an equaliser, and Brian Stein sent the Hatters into raptures with a late winning goal.

Wigan took the Rugby League Challenge Cup trophy again in '88 and '89 with a convincing win over Warrington 36-14 and by a much closer margin of 13-8 over St Helens, closing the decade very much in the way they meant to carry on the next. Joe Lydon, star of the '84 final for Widnes, returned to Wembley, this time for Wigan, having transferred to the Cherry and Whites in '86, and would ultimately be on the winning side with them for five occasions to add to his success with Widnes.

The FA Cup Final of '88 saw yet another appearance by Liverpool, who were dominating both domestic and European football. They were up against Wimbledon who, although a fellow First Division team, were still considered rank outsiders. For Wimbledon it was the culmination of a remark-

The Groundsman's Tale

Often overlooked are the hardworking people behind the scenes, without whom the great sporting events just wouldn't happen. They ensure the pitch is prepared, that lights work, that toilets are maintained – all things we take for granted. At Wembley, one of those people was Joe Power, who worked as a groundsman and later as a Senior Supervisor. Joe came over from Waterford in Ireland in 1963. He was passionate about sport and, while looking for work, was told about the possibility of a job at Wembley. He gave it a try and loved it so much that he stayed for 38 years.

His work involved all aspects of maintaining the pitch, including marking lines and putting in the goalposts for football, hockey or rugby. Yet it was very varied work and his first major event was the 1963 World Speedway Championship, operating the starting gate for each race. More arduous was the installation of the shale speedway track. Thankfully, this only had to be done two or three times a year.

Working at a venue frequented by the stars of sport and music, Joe and his colleagues got to meet a fair number, including England footballers, Jimmy Greaves, Bobby Moore and the Charlton brothers, and pop stars Status Quo, Phil Collins and Rod Stewart. Joe was also there for events such as Live Aid and Euro 96. However, his particular favourites were all in the '60s – West Ham wining the European Cup Winners Cup in 1965 and Manchester United the European Cup in 1968. Top of Joe's list though, not surprisingly, was the 1966 World Cup Final. Joe had also been on duty in 1966 for the infamous England v. Argentina game, when the visitors' captain refused to leave the pitch after being sent off. During the game, one of his tasks was to keep buckets of water topped up. This was usually just for the trainers 'magic sponge' but that day they were needed for cleaning blood from the hallowed turf! In the '90s he was present for some unusual happenings too – the world's biggest ever giant Scrabble game, three helicopters practicing landing on the pitch and seeing the great Pavarotti angered at being drowned out by thunder, lightning and torrential rain during rehearsals for the Three Tenors Concert.

For Joe the only downside was having to work in all weathers. But even this brings back good memories. Despite the best efforts of the ground staff, both the Swindon Town defeat of Arsenal in the 1969 League Cup Final and the draw between Chelsea and Leeds in the 1970 FA Cup Final were played on atrociously muddy pitches. Both turned out to be legendary games. The latter, Joe recalls, included a successful experiment which led to innovations in pitch drainage and a much improved playing surface in subsequent years.

Now retired, Joe looks back on having been able to work at such an enjoyable place for so many years. 'You could see how the players were gripped by the thought that they were playing at Wembley. The place had its own electrifying atmosphere.' Still on Wembley's Christmas card list, Joe is impressed by the new stadium and hopes to get to see a game or two there in the near future.

Wealdstone FC., FA Trophy winners, 1985 (© Wealdstone F.C.)

able journey, which geographically was merely from south to north London, but in historical, football, terms was as good as it could get. The first time they had caused FA Cup headlines was when they were playing in the Southern League thirteen years earlier causing a cup sensation by putting out then First Division Burnley. In just those few years they had risen through the ranks of English football to make the name Wimbledon as synonymous with football as it already was with speedway and tennis.

It has always been the tradition on Cup Final day for neutrals to throw their support behind the underdogs, but for once the football world was divided. Purists of the game disliked Wimbledon's long ball tactics and ruthless approach. Dubbed 'The Crazy Gang' for their dressing room and off-field antics, this team of hard tacklers, such as Vinnie Jones and Dennis Wise, played to their strengths, and effectively so. The footballing artisans of Anfield knew that they shouldn't underestimate their opponents. In an all-red versus all-blue clash, it was Wimbledon who took a surprise first half lead. A long throw into the penalty was headed backwards by Ecuadorian and Irish midfielder Lawrie Sanchez. The ball looped over goalie Grobelaar and in. But there was plenty of time to go, and surely the elegant passing and experience of Liverpool would turn the game around? In the second half a penalty was awarded to Liverpool. No player had ever missed a penalty in a Wembley FA Cup Final. Liverpool's Irish international penalty taker John Aldridge had never missed a penalty – until now. Wimbledon goalkeeper Dave Beasant stood tall then dived heroically to push the ball away, effectively winning the cup for Wimbledon.

For the second year running a new team name was to be engraved on the famous old trophy.

A month later on June 11th there was another huge event at Wembley – the Nelson Mandela 70th Birthday Concert – a marathon ten hour show, with diverse acts that included Joan Armatrading, the Bee Gees, Eric Clapton, Peter Gabriel, Hugh Masakela, Youssou N'Dour, Tears For Fears and Stevie Wonder. Along with the usual 72,000 capacity crowd that were the norm for such events, a billion people around the world watched on television. It was aimed at raising awareness of the thousands in South Africa and Namibia who were imprisoned at the hands of the apartheid regime. Many genres of music could be heard, from jazz to opera via pop and rock, with artists from Africa, North America and Europe performing.

In the eighties Michael Jackson was at his peak and with a stage act that was popular world-wide. So intense was demand for tickets in summer 1988, that he performed at Wembley Stadium for a record-breaking seven sell-out shows, which over half a million people attended. This was part of his 1988 'Bad World' tour featuring his biggest hit singles such as 'Billie Jean', 'Shake Your Body' and 'Don't Stop 'Til You Get Enough'. One show also included a backstage meeting for the singer with the Prince and Princess of Wales.

By the late 1980s Manchester City fans had started a craze of taking giant inflatables to matches. Their inflatable bananas (in homage to their player Imre Varadi) spread, and soon stewards at Wembley Stadium found themselves dealing with fans bringing all sorts of inflatables to matches. Amongst those brightening up the occasion were tigers, whales, and inflatable Silkmen. The Silkmen came courtesy of Macclesfield Town when they contested the 1989 FA Trophy against Telford United, a repeat of the first FA Trophy 29 years earlier. This time, though, Telford scored the only goal.

For a second season in succession Luton Town had another magnificent League Cup run, returning to Wembley, but their ageing side were on the wane and unable to repeat their 1988 triumph. They went down 3-1 to Nottingham Forest, who were picking up their third League Cup, after two successes in the late 1970s.

The tunnel leading onto the sacred turf, late 1980s (© Andy Davidson)

The last FA Cup final of the decade was particularly poignant, coming as it did after the semi final disaster at Hillsborough in Sheffield, when many Liverpool fans lost their lives in a crush at the Leppings Lane end. The city of Liverpool united in grief as Liverpool and Everton contested the final. John Aldridge scored late in the game, only for substitute Stuart McCall to instantly equalise for Everton to force extra time. Liverpool sent on Ian Rush in extra time and he scored twice, and a second from McCall was not enough to save Everton from losing again to their rivals, 3-2. The fences were down at Wembley in response to what had happened at Hillsborough, and there was a small pitch invasion after the game – an out-pouring of emotion rather than anything else.

Evangelist preacher Billy Graham returned to Wembley in 1989. He had packed out the ground back in the 1950s and did so again on his 'Mission 89' tour, as heavy thunderstorms raged all around the Wembley area and to the north beyond, but no lightning struck the famous twin towers.

Inevitably, with such a huge venue as Wembley, records were continually being broken. However, in 1989 an unwanted record was created; that of the lowest attendance for a full England international at Wembley. Only 15,628 turned up to watch the national side play Chile in a Rous Cup game on 23rd May. The small number wasn't a protest by disgruntled fans but a result of a strike by London Underground making it more difficult than usual to get to either of the local tube stations. With the game finishing 0-0 the fans that stayed at home probably didn't feel they'd missed out on anything. The last England international of the decade was a friendly against Yugoslavia. Technically, it was the first all-seater match at the stadium, although with work still being carried out behind the goals converting the stadium, it wasn't exactly in full use and the capacity was temporarily reduced still further. Bryan Robson scored both England goals in a 2-1 win, setting another of his 'fastest goals' records. The Manchester United captain broke his own record set in 1982, this time scoring after 38 seconds, the fastest ever England goal at Wembley.

Wembley Stadium at Legoland, Windsor

1990-2000: When Football Came Home

As a result of the Taylor Report into the Hillsborough disaster, Wembley, as with many other grounds, became an all-seater stadium. This reduced the capacity to 80,000 but improved safety and, to some extent, comfort, although that wasn't a term fans usually associated with a visit to the ageing stadium. Nevertheless, 1990 turned out to be the stadium's peak year in terms of football matches, with a total of 27 played, the same as in the stadium's first nine years put together. Wembley now boasted a very crowded spring schedule with the addition of three league promotion play-off finals as well as the more established fixtures. The play-off finals provided a rare chance for fans of lower league clubs to have their moment of glory, or despair, seeing their heroes have a run out on the hallowed turf. On the other hand some saw this as rather devaluing the Wembley experience, in that a team could finish seventh in the lowest league division and yet still play in a Wembley final. In that first year the sides successfully gaining promotion through this route were Cambridge United (from Division Four), Notts County (from Division Three) and Swindon Town (from Division Two).

In preparation for the Italia '90 World Cup England played a series of friendlies, the most memorable of which was a rare victory over the Brazilians. A goal from Gary Lineker after 37 minutes was the only goal of the game against a side that included Bebeto, Dunga and Branco. The match took place in front of a capacity Wembley crowd, which was a rarity for a friendly. It was in fact the highest attendance for an England match since the Brazilians had last been over for a friendly in 1987. With managers tending to use friendlies increasingly for experimentation, they were often lacking as a spectacle and so fans would vote with their feet.

In the Football League Cup of 1989-90, Nottingham Forest retained the trophy they had won the previous year against Luton Town. This time they achieved a narrow victory over Oldham Athletic. It was Forest and their manager Brian Clough's fourth League Cup triumph. After a promising international career had been cut short by injury, Clough had also taken unfashionable Nottingham Forest to League Championships and European Cups. But with the sun setting on the career of the most successful modern day English manager, the ultimate Wembley prize of the FA Cup still eluded him. Oldham Athletic meanwhile were enjoying the most successful period in their history. Their League Cup final appearance was supplemented by a spell in the top flight and a 1994 FA Cup Wembley appearance. Unfortunately for the Latics, this was a semi-final rather than the final. Their illustrious neighbours Manchester United, inspired by a trademark Mark Hughes volley, put paid to their chances after a replay.

The Rugby League Challenge Cup Final had another torrid tale to tell in 1990 when Wigan's Shaun Edwards played for more than an hour of the match with a broken cheekbone. Wigan, on a roll, still overcame Warrington 36-14, in what was to be the Cheshire side's sixth and final Wembley appearance.

In the first FA Cup Final of the decade, Crystal Palace, in their first ever cup final or Wembley appearance, took on Manchester United, who were seeking their seventh win of the trophy. The fast paced match was tied at 2-2 at the end of the 90 minutes and went into extra-time. Ian Wright, who had only been brought on for the last twenty minutes of normal time as he was not fully fit, put Palace ahead in extra time with his second of the game. However, Mark Hughes grabbed a late equaliser, his second goal of the game, to force a replay. The second game five days later didn't live up to the first. United defender Lee Martin was the unlikely scorer of the only goal as United took the cup back to Old Trafford once again. This was to the great relief of United's manager Alex Ferguson who until then had not delivered any silverware and may otherwise have been seeking alternative employment.

England's 2-1 defeat by Uruguay in May, in another warm up game for Italia '90, was to be goalkeeper Peter Shilton's last international appearance at Wembley. This was a remarkable nineteen and a half years after his England debut, also at Wembley, in November 1970 against East Germany. Earning his 117th cap that night at the age of 40, he went on to reach a total of 125, which remains the record for England to this day. Shilton played under five managers and thirteen captains as well as captaining the side himself on fifteen occasions. The Uruguay game would turn out to be Bobby Robson's last game in charge of the national side at the Twin Towers. He had long suffered at the hands of the tabloid press who were determined to see the back of him, despite a pretty decent track record. Although he went on to lead England through to the World Cup semi-finals in Italy the FA didn't renew his contract and Aston Villa manager Graham Taylor moved into the hot seat.

The high demand for tickets led to a decision to hold the FA Cup semi-final between arch north London rivals Tottenham Hotspur and Arsenal at Wembley in 1991. It made sense as far as crowd size was concerned but at the same time lessened the impact of aiming for the grand Wembley Final. Paul Gascoigne opened the scoring for Spurs with a wonderful strike from a 35 yard free-kick, and Gary Lineker subsequently added two more, as Tottenham went on to overcome The Gunners 3-1. In the final they faced Nottingham Forest, managed by Brian Clough. What should have been the ideal stage for the 23 year old Gascoigne to show off his skills, rapidly turned into disaster. Clearly over-excited by the occasion and lucky not to already have been sent off, he threw himself into a tackle. This resulted in him being stretchered off after only 18 minutes with a serious knee injury that was to keep him out of the game for a year. Forest's captain, Stuart Pearce, made the most of the situation and put his side ahead from the free-kick. Despite this, Gascoigne's team mates levelled the scores in the second half and eventually ran out 2-1 winners in extra-time.

As a warm up for what would prove to be a dismal England performance at Euro '92 in Sweden, they took on France on 19th February 1992. With Graham Taylor at the helm and Stuart Pearce as captain, the 2-0 victory featured the brief overlap of striker Gary Lineker and his ultimate successor, Alan Shearer – both of whom scored that night. Lineker had surprisingly been dropped from the starting eleven and was only brought on as a late substitute. The writing was on the wall and his final Wembley appearance was to come just three months later, which many regarded as very premature.

"Most outstanding of all was that glorious night of May 20, 1992 at the legendary Wembley stadium…" is to this day, how FC Barcelona rated the European Cup Final on its return to the old Wembley for the fifth and final time. The mighty Barcelona were up against Italian side Sampdoria, themselves featuring the talented Lombardo, Vialli and Mancini. Having won the Italian League the previous season for the first time, they were in the middle of the best period the club's history. A crowd of 70, 827 turned out to watch the match, undoubtedly drawn by the chance to see the Barça side dubbed 'The Dream Team'. This was a line up that included Zubizarreta, then Spain's national 'keeper, and Bulgarian Hristo Stoichkov up front. If this were not enough then their coach was Dutchman Johann Cruyff, who had been a legend as a player in his own right. Despite the strength and class of the Catalan side, it took a Ronald Koeman strike deep in extra-time to separate the sides and take the trophy back to the Nou Camp for the first time.

In 1992 another sport was added to the Wembley roll of honour in the form of wrestling. The sport was undergoing a global revival through promotion by the World Wrestling Federation (WWF). The Summer Slam tournament was held in front of an 80,355 crowd, a record for the sport that even beat the high attendances in its traditional USA home.

In October 1992 Great Britain took on Australia in the first Rugby League World Cup Final held at Wembley. In a very hard fought contest, with both sides displaying the strength of their defences, it was the Aussies in the end who came out on top, ten points to six. In a match that was far closer than had been predicted, Britain led 6-4 with just twelve minutes to play. But a try from Steve Renouf was enough to steal the cup for The Kangaroos, despite immense pressure led by St Helens' Gary Connolly and Wigan's Andy Platt for the British side.

Towards the end of the year England's qualifying campaign for the USA '94 World Cup got under way with a disappointing 1-1 draw against Norway, followed by a more convincing 4-0 defeat of Turkey. February 1993 served up one of the perennial whipping boys of Europe's qualifying groups, San Marino. Taking the opportunity to improve their goal difference, England scored six without reply, their biggest victory since 1987. David Platt made the score sheet four times and even missed a penalty, with one each from Carlton Palmer and Les Ferdinand, who was making his debut. The team was brought back to reality in April when a late equaliser gave The Netherlands a 2-2 draw. An important two home points had been dropped.

Arsenal got their revenge on Spurs in a repeat Wembley FA Cup semi-final and so found themselves up against Sheffield Wednesday in the 1993 FA Cup Final. Having beaten The Owls in the League Cup Final just a few weeks earlier, it must have begun to feel like Groundhog Day when the lack-lustre final finished 1-1 and the sides had to meet at Wembley a third time for a replay. Even this game went right down to the wire, with Andy Linighan snatching a 120th minute winner for Arsenal to take the tie 2-1.

With the resumption of USA '94 qualification, despite a further victory against Poland, a promising England side, with Seaman restored after an 18 month interval, suffered poor results away from Wembley, and committed the unforgivable crime of failing to qualify for the World Cup. After a relentless media assault including the infamous turnip caricature by a tabloid newspaper, manager Graham Taylor realised his days were numbered and made his exit. Weeks later in January 1994, Terry Venables, the former Tottenham and Barcelona manager, was in place for what now seemed the

Barcelona celebrate winning the European Cup in 1992. Barca played the match in an orange strip but changed into their traditional shirts to receive the trophy. (© FC Barcelona-Segui)

rather thankless task of managing the national side.

The Rugby League Challenge Cup Final of April 1994 was the best of recent years with Wigan beating Leeds 26-16 to win the trophy for an astonishing seventh time. Wigan's Martin 'Chariots' Offiah stole the day, playing in his third successive final, running almost the length of the field to score the first of his two tries and perhaps the best of his glittering career. Ever present over those seven victories had been the Cherry and White's centre, Dean Bell. Prop forward Andy Platt and second row forward Denis Betts were not far behind, playing in their sixth final. Later in 1994 Rugby League returned to Wembley, this time for the First Test Match between Great Britain and their great rivals Australia. In a tight game, it seemed likely to swing the Aussies' way when Britain's captain Shaun Edwards was sent off in the first half for a dangerously high tackle. But with a try from Widnes (and former Rugby Union) star, Jonathon Davies, it was the Brits who came out unexpected victors by 8-4.

In 1991 and 1992 American Football made a reappearance at Wembley. Riding a brief wave of popularity for the sport, the London Monarchs were founded to participate in the World League of American Football, using Wembley as their home venue. The first season went well with crowds averaging over 40,000, and on the 6th June 1991 the Monarchs won the World Bowl – a play-off between the top two sides at the end of the season, beating Barcelona Dragons 21-0. Unfortunately interest dwindled rapidly and The Monarchs used Wembley for only one more season before working their way through smaller stadia. They were finally disbanded in 1998.

The 1994 Cup Final put a strengthening Chelsea side, under the management of Glenn Hoddle, up against one of the great Manchester United line-ups. The team contained the likes of Peter Schmeichel, Roy Keane, Paul Ince, Ryan Giggs and Mark Hughes, not to mention the cool, arrogant and skilful Frenchman Eric Cantona, at the peak of his powers. After a goalless 60 minutes, Cantona, with his characteristic upturned collar, scored the first of his two from the penalty spot, as Chelsea were swept away 4-0. This not only gave United the trophy for the eighth time but also secured their first league and cup double. Having lost the final to Everton in the intervening year, Manchester United were back in May 1996 for their third consecutive Cup Final. Liverpool were the opposition this time, with a star-strewn line up of their own, notably Steve McManaman, John Barnes, Stan Collymore, Robbie Fowler, Ian Rush and Jamie Redknapp. However, United were stronger than ever. Cantona was back (having been banned after the notorious kung-fu kick at a Crystal Palace fan) and 21 year old

midfielder David Beckham was now established in the first team. That heavily overused term 'classic' could for once be rightly applied to this team. While the game as a whole didn't live up to its potential, it was won in the dying minutes by a piece of Cantona magic. Somehow he volleyed the ball home through a crowded penalty box after Liverpool goalie David James had punched the ball out.

Debuting in a Wembley schoolboy football international in 1995 was a young Englishman with a

bright future, by the name of Michael Owen. Lining up against him for Brazil schoolboys was a promising player who would go on to become a World Cup winner in 2002; Ronaldinho. Owen came out on top that March day, scoring the only goal of the game. He would also score in the June fixture, which was a 2-4 reverse against Germany Schoolboys.

On 2nd September Frank Bruno won Wembley's final boxing bout. The popular Londoner was nearing the end of a successful career, and had narrowly lost at Wembley nine years earlier. In a triumphant homecoming Bruno claimed the World Boxing Council Heavyweight Championship crown, out-pointing American opponent, Oliver 'The Atomic Bull' McCall.

Wembley hosted its second Rugby League World Cup Final on 28th October 1995. Dubbed the Centenary World Cup, it marked the hundredth year of the sport's existence. As with the 1992 competition, Australia met, and again defeated, Great Britain, this time by a slightly more convincing margin of 16-8. It was another hard fought contest, but the best efforts of Farrell, Offiah and Betts couldn't quite match up to Fittler, Johns and Toovey for the Aussies.

1995 saw the beginning of the process that was to end with the closure, demolition and rebuilding of Wembley. The English Sports Council (ESC), was asked to arrange funding and look into the options for an English national stadium. So, even as the creaking Empire Stadium was gearing up for one last major competition, behind the scenes it was already recognised that it was on its last legs. Certainly compared to the newer stadia going up around the world, Wembley was hopelessly out of date, and conditions were poor for the paying public – the fans. The decisions to be taken included whether there should be a major refurbishment or a rebuild, and whether a new stadium should be located at Wembley, or a new site perhaps not even in London? In the debates that arose, some even questioned whether there should be a national stadium at all. After a bidding process, Wembley and Manchester were shortlisted for further consideration.

As part of a mini-tournament called the Umbro

A ticket from the last Wembley concert, August 2000 (Kerry Hegarty)

International Trophy, which was really little more than a series of Euro '96 warm-up games, England once again took on Brazil. Blackburn Rovers' Graeme Le Saux put England ahead in the first half (his only international goal) but unlike 1990 it was the South Americans who came out on top 3-1, through second half goals from Juninho, Edmundo and a teenage Ronaldo, scoring his first international goal. This was England's first home defeat for four years. Three months later there were more South American visitors, as the Colombian national team made their second appearance beneath the Twin Towers in a friendly match in September 1995. A crowd of only 20,000 endured a largely uneventful and goalless game, the main talking point of which was an acrobatic 'scorpion kick' save by the Colombian goalie, Rene Huguita, when he could simply have caught the ball.

Euro '96 was the tenth time that the European Championships (originally called the European Nations Cup) had been held but the first time the finals had taken place in England. Naturally Wembley was the centrepiece, as the venue for the opening ceremony, England's five games and for the final, bringing some much needed excitement and colour to the otherwise dreary and neglected streets of 1990s Brent. Courtesy of the Baddiel, Skinner and Lightning Seeds song 'Three Lions', the tournament will forever be remembered as the time when football came home, with the song being adopted by fans as an England anthem ever since.

Coach Terry Venables had already announced he was vacating the role after Euro '96. His record in charge was excellent but his off-pitch affairs were seen as too much of a distraction, and former Spurs and England favourite Glenn Hoddle was lined up to fill his shoes. This situation, along with the national side's dismal record in the last two major competitions, didn't prevent the usual high expectations. England had never got beyond the semi-finals in this competition over the years but had only been beaten once under Venables, in the friendly against Brazil. The squad was packed with a mix of talent, flair and experience, with David Seaman in goal, Stuart Pearce and Tony Adams in defence and the 'SS' up front; Alan Shearer and Teddy Sheringham. Added to this mix was the potentially brilliant but unpredictable Paul Gascoigne.

8th June saw England, as hosts, get the tournament underway with their group fixture against the Swiss. As now seems to be customary, it was a stuttering start for England, with a 1-1 draw. Seven days later came a very different affair with England up against Scotland for their second group game. In a classic 'Battle of Britain' encounter on a hot summer afternoon, Shearer struck first to put England ahead before half-time. The Scots came close to sinking England's hopes at this early stage in the competition when Adams gave away a penalty midway through the second half. Gary McAllister's spot-kick was saved by Seaman. In the counter attack that sprang from this, Gazza scored a magical, memorable goal, lobbing the ball with exquisite cheek over Hendry in the Scottish penalty box, and volleying past Andy Goram.

Getting their best result in what on paper seemed their hardest game by far, England proceeded to put four past a very strong Netherlands side in their final group game. The Dutch side was dominated by players from Ajax Amsterdam and also included Dennis Bergkamp of Arsenal and Jordi Cruyff of Barcelona, the son of Johann Cruyff. In one of Shearer's greatest games he scored England's first from the penalty spot, and got the third, with Sheringham getting the other two. Patrick Kluivert scored a late consolation goal for the Dutch, but it was England who topped the group to go through to the quarter-final and keep Wembley as their base.

As well as being the first European Championship finals to feature 16 teams, it was also the first major competition to use the Golden Goal method of deciding games in the knock-out phase when scores were level at full-time. This meant that the first goal scored in extra-time would decide the winner, rather

Match ticket from the 1996 European Championsips (Brent Archive)

than playing the full 30 extra minutes. In their quarter-final against Spain, England were lucky to survive with a Spanish goal being disallowed. In the end a tense ninety minutes proved goalless, as did the extra thirty. On this occasion, England's penalty takers proved the more successful, taking the side through 4-2, to lead them through to the inevitable semi-final clash with Germany.

The evening of 26th June 1996 was one of those rare occasions when all but the most die-hard sport haters of the nation were glued to their TV sets for England versus Germany. This was also perhaps the last genuinely classic game at the old stadium. Managed by former West German international, Berti Vogts, this was a side from the now united Germany, following the fall of the Berlin Wall. With the exception of captain and striker Jürgen Klinsmann, at the peak of his career, it wasn't considered an especially formidable German side. Nevertheless, they'd come through what was the toughest group and also beaten a strong Croatia side in the quarter-final. England had never progressed beyond the semi-finals of this competition. Could this be their year? The home nation's hopes remained high and were boosted by the fact that Klinsmann had picked up an ankle injury. Although he was on the bench, realistically he was not going to be used, and instead Andreas Möller took the

captain's armband. As with the 1966 encounter England wore their second strip, which for this season was a mix of blue-grey shades rather than the usual red. In contrast David Seaman sported a very garish red, yellow and mauve kit of a style unfortunately fashionable amongst international 'keepers for a few years.

Unbelievably England went ahead after only two minutes. A strike from distance by Paul Ince forced a punched save from Köpke in the German goal. Shearer scored with a header from the resulting corner. Smiles were soon wiped off English faces when in the fifteenth minute lone-striker Kuntz stole in behind Pearce, preoccupied with appealing for offside, and made it 1-1. The score stayed that way for the rest of the 90 minutes, so the game went into nail-biting extra-time. The Golden Goal rule had everyone on the edge of their seats more than ever, and there were moments when both sides thought they had won it. Kuntz had the ball in the net only for his attempt to be disallowed and Gascoigne came agonisingly close to connecting with a cross from Anderton, with the goal gaping before him. But there was to be no Golden Goal, and once again the result would be down to the lottery of penalties.

With England going first, each side safely scored its first five penalties. The tension was raised to an even higher level as the shoot out went to sudden death. Then came an English management decision easy to question in retrospect, but one that would have been considered brave with a different outcome. Gareth Southgate stepped up next despite being inexperienced at spot-kicks, particularly under such pressure. With a poorly taken penalty he was to be the unfortunate man on this occasion – and there always has to be one – as his penalty was saved. It was left to Germany's captain Möller to seal England's fate by decisively putting away his kick. With Venables already on his way out and England coming within a hair's breadth of making the final, there wasn't too much for the media to criticise. It was after all a great improvement on England's performance in Euro '92, and they hadn't even qualified for USA '94. With his five goal tally, Shearer was to end up as the tournament's top scorer, giving England some minor consolation.

Four days after the host nation's bitter disappointment came the final. Inevitably there was a sense of anti-climax now that England were out, but nonetheless it was a great occasion. Significantly too the FA and Wembley had shown it could successfully host a major international tournament. The Germans, with Klinsmann now restored to the team but without the suspended Möller, were seeking their third tournament win (the previous two were as West Germany). The Czech Republic having scraped through Group C behind the Germans, were seeking their second (the first being as part of the former Czechoslovakia, against West Germany in 1976). Their side included Karel Poborsky, Patrik Berger, Vladimir Smicer and Pavel Nedved, all on their way to becoming household names in the UK. After Berger put the Czechs ahead with a 58th minute penalty it was Oliver Bierhoff, brought on as a substitute for the last twenty minutes, who equalised and saved the day for the Germans. Another game was to go into extra-time. And after just four minutes it was Bierhoff who grabbed the first Wembley Golden Goal and gave Germany victory.

Glenn Hoddle's first game in charge at Wembley in October 1996 seemed to carry on from where Venables had left off. Shearer scored twice as England beat Poland 2-1 in a World Cup qualifier. Having made his international debut five weeks

earlier, the game was also the first Wembley appearance of David Beckham. With only a subsequent 1-0 setback at home to Italy, this was to prove a successful campaign for Hoddle and England qualified for the France '98 World Cup.

The future, or not, of Wembley became slightly clearer in December 1996 with the ESC decision to select it over Manchester as the preferred site for a new stadium. £120m of lottery funding would also be put towards the project. It seemed that the benefits of remaining in the nation's capital, plus the established brand name of Wembley, had sufficiently outweighed the prospect of a cheaper Manchester site and starting afresh with public transport (which had long been a source of much aggravation in north-west London). As the Empire Stadium now entered its final straight, the world outside Britain was again changing. After eighteen years of Conservative governments, John Major lost the 1997 General Election to Labour's Tony Blair. Brit-pop filled the airwaves whilst musicians and artists mingled, perhaps unwisely, with politicians, and the concept of 'Cool-Britannia' was born.

Between them Manchester United and Arsenal dominated 1990s domestic football. In the 1998 Cup Final Arsenal beat Newcastle United 2-0, to achieve the club's second league and cup double. A year later Manchester United added to Alan Shearer and The Toon Army's misery with The Magpies again on the wrong end of a 2-0 score-line. Despite many promising FA Cup runs in a record-breaking career, Shearer was never to get nearer a winner's medal at Wembley than this. It could be argued that Manchester United's line-up that season,

Wembley Speedway memorabilia (© Andy Davidson)

Iestyn Harris, captain of Leeds Rhinos, winners of the 1999 Rugby League Challenge Cup (© Leeds Rhinos RFC)

including the great Dane Peter Schmeichel in goal, Gary Neville, David Beckham, Paul Scholes, Roy Keane, Teddy Sheringham, Ryan Giggs and Ole-Gunnar Solskjaer was the best in its illustrious history. Now taking the cup for the tenth time, this also completed another double, which would turn into an astonishing historic treble when they won the Champions League shortly afterwards.

As they tried to keep pace with the higher income and spending power of their northern rivals, Arsenal had been feeling the limitations of their Highbury ground. The club put in an extravagant bid to purchase Wembley stadium, which was turned down. Arsenal then sought, and obtained, permission to use the stadium as their home venue for the Champions League group phase in 1998 and 1999. Despite the extra capacity, it was to prove a failure on the pitch, with two wins, a draw and three defeats in the two seasons, and they switched back to Highbury after that. Many fans felt that the brave and ingenious experiment had failed partly as the crowd were unable to recreate the atmosphere generated at Highbury on European nights.

December 1998 saw the end of greyhound racing at Wembley after 71 years. Falling attendances had made it increasingly uneconomical and there were enough alternative and viable venues to meet the punters' demand. Greyhound racing had been the bread and butter income for Wembley for many years, and had a long, successful and proud history at the venue. But all good things must come to an end, a proverb that the very stadium itself was about to experience the reality of.

England manager Glenn Hoddle's spell in charge came to an unfortunate end through a combination of mixed results in the Euro 2000 qualifiers, and some bizarre and unwise public utterings about disability being a punishment for wrong-doings in previous lives. What followed was to turn out to be equally unfortunate and unwise as, on a wave of media-led popularity, Kevin Keegan was ushered in early in 1999. Seen as a great man motivator, initially the change did bring some success. In Keegan's first game in charge at Wembley in March, a Paul Scholes hat-trick brought a 3-1 victory over the Poles.

Having been set up two years earlier as a wholly owned subsidiary of the FA, in March 1999 Wembley National Stadium Limited (WNSL) bought Wembley Stadium for £103 million from Wembley plc. WNSL's role would be to oversee the design and financing of the new Wembley, and to operate it on completion of the build. At this stage it was still felt that the twin-towers were certain to remain whatever else happened.

In the meantime, Wembley became part of Wales in early 1999. With Cardiff's new Millennium Stadium under construction, Wembley became a temporary home for the Wales Rugby Union Five Nations Championship matches. In their match versus England the Welsh came away happiest with a 32-31 point victory. The last Wembley final of the Rugby League Challenge Cup was held on 1st May 1999. Leeds Rhinos won the trophy for the first time in 21 years by beating London Broncos, who were in their first final, 52-16. A try from former Wigan star Martin Offiah, in the autumn of his playing career, couldn't prevent the Broncos being on the wrong side of the highest score and biggest winning margin in a final. However, getting this far was an achievement for the London side in only their nineteenth year of existence. Rhinos captain, Iestyn Harris scored eight goals and one try, but the man of the match, playing the game of his life, was Leroy Rivett with an incredible four tries. In getting his fourth Rivett also became the scorer of the last ever try at the old Wembley.

Bolton Wanderers, who graced Wembley in its early days, also played there in the stadium's last years. Their third Wembley play-off final ended with a 2-0 defeat to Watford in the 1999 battle for a premiership place. The most fascinating play-off final for many a year also took place that weekend. Kent's only league team, Gillingham, were enjoying a rise in their fortunes, coinciding with the fall from the top of Manchester City. They met in the Division Two final. For City even a win would only have meant promotion to a division they still felt was beneath them, whereas for the Gills it would have been ground-breaking. It was Gillingham who took control, and more importantly a two-goal lead. For City it was the lowest in the league they had ever sunk, and looked like they would have to spend a second year there. Out of nowhere they turned the match around with two late goals, and then kept their nerve to win promotion 3-1 on penalties. Gillingham endured a year of heart-break before returning to the last play-offs at Wembley in 2000. Against Wigan Athletic they won another exciting encounter, by three goals to two after extra time. A day later the final Wembley play-off saw Ipswich Town defeat Barnsley 4-2 for a place in the Premiership.

The Wembley-based play-off finals that commenced at the start of the decade produced some memorable games. This method of promotion at the last chance saloon produced some very close and tense matches, as well as some highly frenetic ones. The first to require the ubiquitous penalties was in 1991 when Torquay United beat Blackpool 5-4 in the Division Four play-off. A year later Blackpool were back, to turn penalty shoot-out agony into ecstasy, as they beat Scunthorpe United 4-3. Two high-scoring play-offs were the 1993 Swindon Town 4-3 victory over Leicester City and Bolton Wanderers' win over Reading by the same score-line in 1995. Highest scoring of all was the 4-4 draw between Charlton Athletic and Sunderland in 1998. In a see-saw match, fans and players of both sides had periods when they felt they were going into the Premiership, only to see their hopes dashed.

Leroy Rivett scores a try for Leeds Rhinos (© Leeds Rhinos RFC)

Eventually it went to penalties, and sudden–death. Charlton scraped through 7-6 on penalties.

A 6-0 win over Luxembourg in a Euro 2000 qualifier in September 1999, including a Shearer hat-trick, could not offset other indifferent results and the poor start inherited from Hoddle. England therefore failed to quality automatically but did just enough to get a final chance through a two-legged play-off. As fate would have it, this brought England up against the Scots for a chance to appear in the finals. This was a much welcomed encounter after the ending of the home internationals in the 1980s had made the fixture a rarity. England brought a 2-0 advantage back from Hampden Park for the home leg in November. However, the Scots unexpectedly embarrassed the English at Wembley pulling off a 1-0 win through a Don Hutchinson goal late in the first half. But this was not enough to prevent England squeezing through 2-1 on aggregate.

2000 was the final year of active service for the Empire Stadium (although it would eventually be February 2003 before demolition was completed). The FA Cup semi-finals were back at the twin towers again and at this stage Bolton Wanderers came close to completing a sort of symmetry. Having won the first Wembley final in 1923, it would perhaps have been romantic for them to win the last. But romance was not on Aston Villa's minds and they put Bolton out, although this took extra-time and penalties. In the final Villa were up against Chelsea's increasingly multinational line up, now

Inside the old Wembley Stadium

under the management of Italian Gianaluca Vialli. Making this something of an Italian job, his countryman Roberto Di Matteo scored the only goal of a largely disappointing game to close the era of Wembley Cup Finals. A more lasting impact was made by Chelsea's captain Dennis Wise who collected the trophy with his four month old son Henry in his arms, decked out in matching Chelsea kit. It probably wasn't what Dennis had on his mind at the time, but this was seen as capturing something of the changing nature of men in British society, with Dennis wanting to be seen sharing his proudest moment with his child.

The stadium's status as a major music venue was undiminished in its final decade with INXS, Michael Jackson, U2 and Oasis all performing to football sized crowds. INXS described the gig as 'the biggest pub we've ever played'. Other summer gigs included the Christian 'Champion of the World' concert in 1997, and the Net Aid charity concert in

Stage set for The Spice Girls Concert, 1998 (© Joe Power)

1999 featuring David Bowie.

American rock band Bon Jovi had the honour of performing the last two concerts in the stadium on the 19th and 20th August 2000 as part of their 'Crush' tour. Their final song on the final night could have been on behalf of the old stadium itself, entitled 'Thank You for Loving Me'. As a 17 year old in the crowd that night, Londoner Kerry Hegarty was at her first ever gig having become a Bon Jovi convert with the 'Crush' album. *'The atmosphere was electric when they came on. Although Jon's white suit was a bit tacky and didn't go with the rock 'n' roll image, he really lit up the stage. Our seats were expensive at £55 but we had a good view of the stage from the stands. It looked fun to be down in the pitch area. I would have loved to have been down there too for a while. We knew it was the last gig at the stadium and it seemed like an excellent way to say farewell to Wembley'.*

7th October 2000 could and should have been the great grand finale for Wembley. The last fixture could not have been more appropriate; England v. Germany in a World Cup Qualifier, with an England team containing some of the best players in the world at the time, such as Seaman, Beckham, Adams and Owen. What transpired though was the most disjointed and inept England performances for many years. The only goal of the game, and therefore the last goal to ever be scored at the old stadium, was from a free-kick by Germany's Dietmar Hamann. Manager Keegan resigned shortly after the end of the match. A very likeable and honest man who didn't hide his feelings, he bravely came out and stated what many already felt, that he wasn't up to the job.

After Keegan's managerial demise and an endless debate, a non-English, non-British manager was handed the England job – Sven Goran Eriksson, a Swede who had built a great reputation as manager of Italian club, Lazio. His entire managerial episode was to take place during Wembley's rebuilding years however, and so is a story to be told elsewhere. With the much longer gap than anyone had anticipated between the old and new stadiums being in use, many more international careers came to an end in the meantime. As a result, the October 2000 game would be the last

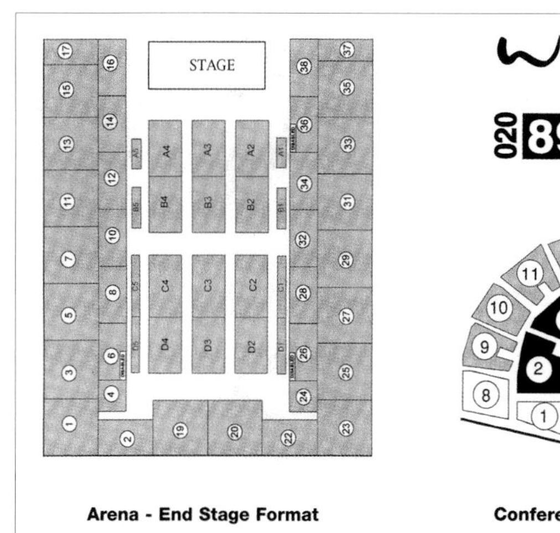

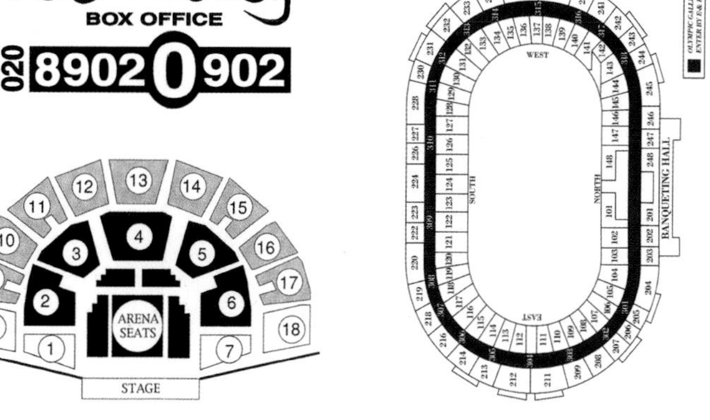

**Event seat plans, venue & travel information, event search and listing facilities plus on-line booking
www.wembleyticket.com**

Seating Plans for Wembley Stadium, Arena and Conference Centre

Wembley appearance for David Seaman, Paul Scholes and Gareth Southgate. It may also have been the last Wembley run out, in an England shirt at least, for David Beckham, and perhaps even for the increasingly injury prone Michael Owen.

The player who will forever hold the record for the most appearances at the old Wembley is Tony Adams, with a total of 60, closely followed by Peter Shilton with 58. A stalwart of the famous Arsenal back-four of the late '80s and '90s, Adams led his side to FA Cup Final successes in '93 and '98 plus League Cup victories in '87 and '93. Tony made a total of 36 Wembley appearances for England, including sixteen as captain, most notably during the Euro 96 campaign. His total reflects a hugely successful career for both club and country, but was also boosted by several of Arsenal's cup semi-finals being held at Wembley, along with The Gunners using the twin towers as their home venue for two seasons in the Champions League and three years of pre-season friendly tournaments.

Adam's first England appearance at Wembley was in May 1987 in a friendly against Brazil. Appropriately, his last Wembley appearance was as the England captain in the stadium's farewell fixture – the World Cup Qualifier versus Germany in October 2000.

The end is nigh for the twin towers, February 2003

Following England's defeat by Germany, the Empire Stadium closed its doors for the last time. After seventy-seven and a half glorious years, only the echoes and ghosts of the Cup Finals, England triumphs and disasters, Live Aid and so much more were left drifting round the empty stands of this aging arena. Whether fans had come away celebrating, or with their hopes dashed, or simply having been glad to witness a great event, it was a place that meant so very much to so many people. Now, of course, we all hoped the stadium to come in its place would make us feel the same. At this point the target date for reopening was the 2003 FA Cup Final. In the interim the major finals would be switched to the Millennium Stadium, in the Welsh capital, Cardiff, while England's home games would be at various club grounds.

Not long after closing, the pitch was removed and auctioned off in 30,000 pieces. Thousands of other items were also auctioned off, from corner flags to photos and even a cardboard cut-out of Sir Stanley Matthews. A few weeks later the outside was cordoned off ready for the arrival of the bulldozers. Anyone taking a last look now could see that it was well past its use-by date and certainly not what you'd expect from a major 21st century venue. After all, it was a 1920s idea of a multi-sports arena that hadn't been designed for such a long and varied life. Having been built in the early days of radio, let alone television, it was from an age when expectations were very different and going to an event was virtually the only way to experience it.

The twin towers still looked magnificent but their fate was by now sealed. Although the stadium as a whole had the veil of protection of being a Grade 2 Listed Building, the scale of any new project would mean the towers were simply in the way. Although some local councillors originally wanted to insist that the towers were kept as a condition for approving the new stadium, the argument was lost. In the end Brent Council gave approval for their demolition and there was no objection from English Heritage. It has to be said that it was only the twin towers that a lot of people wanted kept. The rest of the structure was not going to be missed! Sadly the way the towers had been constructed meant that it would have been prohibitively expensive to attempt to move them. It may have come down to a choice between keeping the towers or having a new stadium on the site, rather than the ideal of both. Public opinion had been split between on the one hand seeing it as vital to keep the towers for their appearance and the significance the nation attached to them, and on the other hand, not letting nostalgia get in the way of progress. It's hard to say whether we'll ultimately regret this. However, the towers were of such significance that questions were asked in the House of Commons as to why the demolition was to be permitted.

A makeshift pitch was actually put back to cater for the filming of the match scenes in the movie *Mike Bassett: England Manager*, starring Ricky Tomlinson in the title role. Only a few hundred extras were used for the crowd scenes inside Wembley, so clever editing and computer trickery had to be used for the finished version.

In September 2000, after a joint bid from Bovis and Multiplex was turned down, a Multiplex offer to build the new stadium for £326.5m was accepted by WNSL. Documents revealed several years later seemed to indicate that plans at that stage were still somewhat vague. This would later be at the core of disputes as to what exactly was being bid for and agreed at that stage. WNSL, under the Chairmanship of Chelsea owner Ken Bates, then appointed Multiplex as contractors for the project. The bid was seen as being good value for WNSL and came hot on the heals of Multiplex's highest profile project to date – the Sydney Olympic Stadium – a magnificent stadium built on time for a highly successful Olympic Games.

Demolition of sorts began late in 2000 but rapidly came to a halt. Financial backing for the project remained problematic and for a while even seemed in danger of falling through. Matters were

One of the old Wembley entrances, November 2000

TURNSTILE
D

complicated by the new Sports Minister, Kate Hoey, appearing to reopen decisions that had already been settled over the athletics track issue and even the twin towers. The local authority Brent Council were also involved in arguments over contributions to the upgrading of the local transport infrastructure, particularly Wembley Park tube station. The end result was an increasingly derelict looking, unused stadium and a lot of people wondering if the closure had been horribly premature.

In February 2001, with the future of Wembley in turmoil, Ken Bates resigned from WNSL. As well as feeling immense frustration with the bankers, Chase Manhattan, he expressed considerable anger at what he saw as a lack of backing from others within WNSL and the relevant government ministers. By early May, the media was still full of bleak reports on the prospects of ever getting a new Wembley built but by the end of the month, miraculously, the FA were announcing that the project was back on course – a loan having been secured through German bank, Westdeutsche Landesbank. With the change of chairmanship, aspects of the plans were re-thought. Proposals for a hotel and office complex were dropped, and in their place, as a potential major income generating scheme, came Club Wembley – the ultimate upmarket package. This consists of 17,000 of the best seats which, for a substantial licence fee and annual instalments, are yours for ten years. This would be in addition to the 166 executive boxes costing upwards of £65,000 per year for eight to twenty people.

It still took until September the following year for a final deal to be resolved with Multiplex but in November 2002 demolition got under way for real. The new completion date was set as January 2006, to be ready in time for the May 2006 FA Cup Final. It was a time of mixed emotions – optimism and relief that things were at last moving forwards but sadness that the twin towers' days were numbered. Wembley, as a town, had been in steady decline for years. Unwary fans expecting a town that matched the glamour of the sporting occasions were met either by the very missable Wembley High Road on one approach or the once infamous Chalkhill Estate on the other! A major regeneration centred on the stadium was much needed.

As well as the involvement of a German bank in financing the new Wembley there was some further German involvement at the demolition stage. A specially designed 130 tonne machine, nicknamed 'Goliath', was brought in for the work. Made by German company Liebharr it was designed to have a 35 metre reach allowing it to get to the highest parts of the towers, and to be able to use interchangeable attachments – one a concrete pulveriser, the other a shearer.

The World Stadium Team Consortium were appointed as architects for the new stadium. This combined Australian Rod Sheard of HOK Sport, responsible for Cardiff's Millennium Stadium and the Sydney Olympic Stadium, with British architect Sir Norman Foster, responsible for Stansted Airport, London's City Hall, Millennium Bridge and Swiss Re tower (better known as 'The Gherkin'). The aim of this mighty partnership was to build a stadium to not only provide the best for fans and for modern media coverage but to also create an iconic building to aid regeneration of the surrounding area.

The total cost of the project was to be £757m to cover land purchase, demolition and design fees, as well as building and fitting out the new stadium. Its capacity would be 90,000 with each seat offering more legroom than even the old stadium's Royal Box. There would be two giant TV Screens, 30 escalators, 688 food points, 13 restaurants, over 2,500 toilets and 400 media seats. Facilities for players would also include a small practice pitch.

The design team came up with an interesting way to resolve one of the on-going debates about what should be in the new building. Whilst the new stadium was to be primarily for football, rugby and music, the design would also incorporate a removable athletics track. This would by-pass the usual problem that having a permanent track pushes the crowd back an excessive distance from the action. Having the track installed would reduce capacity to 70,000 and need the closure of the stadium for several weeks before and after but it would enable Wembley to bid for a wider range of major events.

7th February 2003 was the day many people thought they would never witness. It was the day when demolition of the twin towers themselves began. With it being a weekday and the event just being publicised the day before, only around a

November 2000: A turnstile, definitely showing its age

It's nearly all over for the twin towers, 7th February 2003

thousand people came to witness this momentous occasion, along with numerous TV crews. After much standing around, a minor ceremony and some barely audible announcements, the 'Goliath' machine moved across and began nibbling away at one of the towers' domes. As an event it was rather an anti-climax, as little more was achieved that afternoon. In fact the drill on the end of the machine's arm looked strangely inappropriate, scraping away at the dome with the same effect as someone trying to eat soup with a fork!

The bulk of the demolition of the beloved towers was, in the end, spread agonisingly across the next five days but with only local office workers and handfuls of dedicated fans to witness it. By the 12th February it was finally all over and there was just rubble and mud left, except for one section of stand on the southern side, which was also to vanish shortly afterwards.

Several features of the stadium were saved by the *Brooking Collection of Architectural Detail*, set up by Charles Brooking in the 1960s. When the Collection first approached Wembley for access to the stadium before demolition, they found themselves in competition with the many fans clamouring for mementoes. However, endorsement from English Heritage, itself keen to preserve a number of features, ensured that the request was granted. The Collection is well known and used by the architects and conservationists as a unique reference resource for items such as doors, windows and balustrades. For Brooking, there was also a sentimental interest. *'Wembley Stadium was built by the grandfather of the current Chairman of my Collection's Trustees,'* he explained, *'so I just had to acquire some of those iconic pieces, for Sir William McAlpine's sake'.*

Whilst the stadium was being carefully stripped of dangerous materials such as asbestos, Charles and assistant Wendy spent 18 months identifying elements to save. After going up inside the twin towers, Brooking found that whilst they looked grand from the outside, inside they were very utilitarian. *'They were built in situ, the concrete walls being poured into a timber mould. The interior of the walls remained unadorned, just as when they were constructed in 1923. You could clearly see where each day's concrete level finished and the next*

began. No wonder they found it impossible to take the towers down and re-instate them elsewhere. When they came to be broken up, the walls broke irregularly like a huge Easter egg. It was a great shame to see them go, but inevitable.'

They also discovered things few fans would have known – one tower was an electrical switching room, the other a storage area for club banners and tapes of the national anthems of the various teams who had played there. When the flagpoles were removed they also discovered something that no-one seemed to know, that on top of each tower was a gilded crown. These became the first items to join the collection. Also recovered were smaller features, including the doors and bay window of the Royal Retiring Room and many notable windows from the stadium's offices and the unusual circular ones from the twin towers. Behind the Royal Box, two layers of plywood were found to be concealing the most elaborate Chinoiserie patterned doors embellished with imitation tortoiseshell and lacquer: a neo-classical design by leading architect Maxwell Ayrton, it had been hidden since the modifications of 1948 and 1989. Elegant door furniture from the magnificent entrance doors to the Great Hall was also recovered, as were some of the elaborate fanlight windows from the Long Bar.

When it came to the massive doors from the Royal Tunnel, part of the impressive façade that used to greet visitors to the stadium, their removal had to wait until after much of the site had been levelled. Weighing in at several tons and measuring 17x15 feet, specialist transport had to be provided and roads closed to accommodate their journey to storage in Kettering.

November 2000: The old stadium with demolition imminent

November 2000

November 2000: With the pitch now removed, the bulldozers were ready to roll

November 2002: On a stadium tour

Winter 2002/3: Demolition of the stands progresses rapidly

Early 2003: The South Stand

January 2003: The demolition as viewed from nearby offices

January 2003: The remaining stretch of the façade between the towers

January 2003: What was left resembled a ruined fortress rather than a stadium

January 2003: Just the towers and parts of the north and south stands remain

By late January 2003, little was left but the towers

7th February 2003: An England fan with a replica of the Jules Rimet Trophy, the World Cup, as won in 1966

7th February 2003: The day the demolition of the towers began

July 2005: The arch is lit up to mark London's successful Olympic bid

9

2003-2007: The Rise of the New

We'd hardly had time to wipe away the tears when the new building started to rise from the mud and rubble of the old. It wasn't a lot to look at at first but if it ended up looking like the computer generated images that had been appearing in the press, it would be spectacular. The lines of cranes looming over the rooftops of Wembley, and the rapidly rising towers that would house the lifts and staircases, signalled that the north-west London skyline would soon be dramatically changed.

As a spectacular feature to, in a sense, take the place of the towers, there would be an imposing arch. With a span of 315 metres and a height of 133 metres, it would be big enough to fit the London Eye underneath. It would be moveable but would generally be fixed at an angle of 68 degrees. But it was not simply eye-catching, it would also be functional, supporting the whole of the north roof and 60% of the weight of the south, avoiding the need for pillars and ensuring no restricted view seats.

The stadium's design also aimed to solve a problem that newer roofed stadia had been encountering – that the pitch doesn't get enough sunlight or air for the grass to grow properly, resulting in frequent, expensive replacements. The design therefore incorporates a retractable roof on the south side. This can be opened to lessen the amount of shadow across the pitch and also allows for clearer TV pictures. And if that isn't enough, the quality of the pitch, four metres lower than the old one, will also be maintained by a system of ducts that can supply warm air if needed or suck out any excess moisture.

In October 2003 work was clearly progressing well on the arch. It was being constructed in sections flat on the ground, with these sections then welded together. By December the final sections were being assembled.

In April 2004, with the arch completed on the ground, giant cranes were moved into place ready to lift it. The raising was delayed, however, after it was found that some welds were not strong enough. The delay was not too serious though and in May it was slowly lifted into place.

The generally grim weather of that May was replaced by a sunnier June, and while England football fans enjoyed the teams exploits in Euro 2004 in Portugal, the gleaming new arch could now dominated the skyline from every approach. It seemed to indicate that the project as a whole was going well and on schedule. It became an instant new icon for London. As the feature that really gives the stadium something unique, it's interesting to note that it wasn't even in the early plans, which instead had a series of giant masts!

As the months passed, work focused more on the main structure of the building and the banking for the seating areas. Instead of the four separate stands of the old stadium, the new Wembley is arranged as one complete 'bowl', rising higher than before and much closer to the pitch. As well as improved sightlines for all parts of the crowd and more comfortable seats with more legroom, the architects even went as far as to use computer modelling to try to emulate the acoustics of the old Wembley, so as not to lose the atmosphere.

In February 2005, with less than a year to go to the completion deadline, the International Olympic Committee visited Wembley, on a whistle-stop tour of all the sites that would hold events if London was awarded the 2012 Olympic Games. Although Wembley will only hold the latter stages of the football competitions, there was more to see there than at most of the other potential event venues, which were still at the planning stage. Over the coming weeks and months though, alarm bells began to sound about the project being delayed. At this stage however, the construction company still maintained that it would be ready for the FA Cup Final in May 2006.

In July that year London was awarded the 2012 Olympics. While most headed to celebrations in Trafalgar Square, a few headed to Wembley where the arch was illuminated to mark the success. While this came across as a statement of confidence in the stadium – and from the outside, it was looking good – the following months were to reveal the true situation. At first the deadline for Multiplex to handover the completed stadium was put back from January to March 2006. There were also announcements that the project would go over budget, though, with it being a fixed price contract, Multiplex would take the hit. Yet they still seemed confident that the new stadium would host the 2006 FA Cup Final as planned, and concerts and England friendlies were also being lined up. Press reports in February then suggested that all was not so rosy on the inside, with problems of rain penetration into parts of the building along with plumbing and design problems in the shower areas.

> In 2005 a bronze sculpture of Bobby Moore, England's 1966 World Cup winning captain, was commissioned by WNSL, to take pride of place outside the main entrance of the new stadium. Award winning sculptor, Philip Jackson, was chosen to create the piece. His previous work includes the statues of Sir Matt Busby which is outside Old Trafford, 'The Champions' (Moore, Hurst etc) near West Ham United's ground and Queen Elizabeth II, in Windsor Great Park.

In March 2006 the new White Horse Bridge was approaching completion, put together by Cleveland Bridge, the same company who constructed the stadium's arch. Named in honour of the police horse that helped clear the pitch for the first Wembley Cup Final in 1923, this was to provide an attractive, direct link between Wembley High Road and the stadium, with up to 7,000 people an hour expected to cross it on event days. The name, which was chosen through a ballot organised by the London Development Agency and BBC Radio Five Live, was a surprising choice in the end, beating Alf Ramsey, Geoff Hurst and Bobby Charlton. There had also been an attempt at hijacking the vote by some Scottish fans who wanted the

bridge named after Jim Baxter, captain of their '67 side that defeated the English at Wembley.

But the positive news about the bridge couldn't counter the unfolding bad news. That same month the FA found themselves having to announce that they were switching the FA Cup Final to Cardiff for one more year – Multiplex couldn't guarantee that Wembley would be ready in time. Weeks later, as more problems surfaced and the cost overrun estimate rocketed to £183 million, all planned events for 2006 were called off or moved to other venues. The delay was to be a full year. Of course, all this provided fodder for media, ever hungry for stories of embarrassment and scandal in high profile projects – and you couldn't get a higher profile than this. In the end though, it was the only rational decision the FA could take. It was clearly better to have a magnificent, safely built stadium than one where corners have been cut to save money or meet an artificial deadline. A few matches and gigs in, fans will simply not care about the delay, as has been the case for other major projects in the past

By this time, behind the scenes disputes were developing between Multiplex and WNSL that looked as though they could take a long time to resolve. WNSL believed that they had an agreement that Multiplex would bear any cost overruns, while Multiplex believed that WNSL had made so many changes to the plans that it had become impossible to work to the original cost and schedule. While the work carried on, mixed PR messages continued to emanate from the project. In May 2006 there was the sight of the current England squad having a kick-about in the new stadium – albeit on sand where the pitch would be. A month later, while the sporting world was transfixed by the World Cup in Germany and the saga of Wayne Rooney's metatarsal, Wembley announced the laying of the first strips of turf for the new pitch. Laying the whole playing surface – some 10,000m^2 – would take a full week. In between the morsels of good news came the unexpected and disappointing announcement by Multiplex that they couldn't guarantee that the stadium would be ready for the 2007 FA Cup Final, though this was probably more to do with managing expectations than because of further lengthy delays.

In July 2006 WNSL announced that they now

believed that it was unlikely that the stadium would be handed over to them by September 2006 – the latest provisional deadline. However, they were confident it would be completed by the end of the year. It was clear how poor the relationship had become between the parties when, almost simultaneously, Multiplex themselves were saying the delay would be even longer but that this was due to certain vital tasks not being carried out by WNSL.

October 2006 brought media speculation of further delays and the disappointment of Wembley failing in its bid to host either the 2008 or 2009 European Champions League Finals. But, out of the gathering gloom, just a couple of weeks later came the very positive news that WNSL, The FA and Multiplex had reached a deal over the cost overruns. In order to avoid a potentially lengthy and expensive legal dispute, the parties had come to a timely compromise. There would also be a new financial incentive for Multiplex to ensure the stadium was ready for the 2007 FA Cup Final. With it said to be 95% complete at this point, the FA were now confident that Wembley would open at some point in 2007, although they didn't specify exactly when! However, with plans being pencilled in to hold two smaller 'test' events (a requirement of the local authority before the stadium gets its licence to hold full capacity events) things were finally looking genuinely optimistic.

By the end of the year the signs were unmistakably good as events were announced for the summer onwards and tickets put on sale. First came the news that British rock band, Muse, would headline two dates in mid-June 2007. A few days later came the announcement of the 'Concert for Diana' in July, a major charity event organised by Princes William and Harry, featuring Sir Elton John, Duran Duran and Bryan Ferry. For both events, tickets were snapped up at an incredible rate. Shortly after, keeping up the Wembley tradition of hosting a diverse range of events, The Race of Champions was announced for the following December. This would feature top drivers from Formula One, NASCAR and the Le Mans Rally and require the construction of a temporary motor racing circuit within the stadium.

Finally, January 2007 brought the news that every-

one had been waiting for. With only relatively minor work left to be completed, the new Wembley would be ready in time to host the 2007 FA Cup Final. The stage was now set not only for the return of the Cup Final to its traditional home, but also England's qualifiers and friendlies, the League Cup and Play-Off Finals, Rugby Leagues Challenge Cup Final and summers of major rock concerts.

So, a big 'thank you' to Cardiff and Old Trafford for standing in, but Wembley – a magnificent, new and better than ever Wembley – is back in business!

Summer 2003: Early stages of the new stadium

Autumn 2003: The new stadium rises from the rubble of the old

Autumn 2003

October 2003: Early stages of the construction of the arch

December 2003: The final sections of the arch are assembled

April 2004: The arch is completed and cranes are moved in ready to lift it

April 2004

May 2004: The arch is slowly lifted into place

May 2004

June 2004: The arch is in place as the focus of England fans turns to Euro 2004

June 2004: The new arch, shortly after being lifted into place

The stadium viewed from Stonebridge Park

October 2004: Arch and cranes

The arch reflected in a Wembley Park hotel

February 2005: The outer structure is now fleshed out

May 2005: With one year to the proposed re-opening, the work seemed to be going well

July 2005: As daylight fades the arch lights begin to show

May 2005: The new stadium from Olympic Way

May 2005: The new White Horse Bridge approaches completion

July 2005: The new arch in all its illuminated glory as London celebrates being awarded the 2012 Olympics

November 2006: New Wembley from Sherrins Farm Open Space

OLD WEMBLEY v. NEW WEMBLEY

EMPIRE STADIUM		ENGLISH NATIONAL STADIUM
1922	**Started**	2003
1923	**Completed**	2007
£750,000	**Cost**	£757m (+£183m overspend)
127,000 at opening 100,000 from 1950-1989 76,000 at close	**Capacity**	90,000
23,000 at opening 100,000 from 1950-1989 76,000 all seater at close	**Seated**	90,000
8,100 seats	**Restricted View**	Nil
66cms	**Seat Depth**	80cms
38.4m (Towers)	**Stadium Height**	133m (Arch)
68 x 105 metres	**Pitch size**	68 x 105 metres
356	**Toilets**	2,588
5	**Disabled Toilets**	30
152	**Food Points**	688
2	**Restaurants**	13
2	**Escalators**	30
0	**Lifts**	26
162	**Media Seats**	400

A Wembley Timeline

10

767   Earliest record of land in Wembley

825   Earliest reference to Wemba Lea (meaning 'Wemba's Clearing')

1851   Wembley's population is recorded as 209 with the area still mostly fields and farms

1895   First stage of Watkin's Tower completed (on the site of the future Stadium) and opened

1901   Watkin's Tower closed

1907   Watkin's Tower demolished

1913   Wembley chosen as 1924 British Empire Exhibition site, to include a major new sports stadium

1921   The Football Association (FA) declare their interest in the new stadium as their current Cup Final venue, Stamford Bridge, is too small for the crowds

1922   Work commences on new 'Empire Stadium'

1923   Building is completed ready for following year's Empire Exhibition but the first event held is the FA Cup Final, Bolton Wanderers 2 West Ham 0 ('The White Horse Final')

1924   British Empire Exhibition held in Wembley, including the new stadium. First football international: England 1 Scotland 1

1927   Welsh club Cardiff City win the (English) FA Cup, beating Arsenal, taking the trophy outside England for first time. Arthur Elvin buys stadium for £122,500. First greyhound racing held

1929   First Rugby League Challenge Cup Final at Wembley: Wigan beat Dewsbury 13-2. First speed way at Wembley: Wembley Lions set up, using the stadium as their home venue

1934   First baseball played at stadium between teams from U.S. forces.

1936   First World Speedway Championships

1940   Dunkirk evacuees sheltered at stadium

1942   Rugby Union first played at Wembley, with England beating Scotland

1945   England draw 2-2 with France in an unofficial first football international (other than against a 'Home' nation) at Wembley

1948   London Olympics. Wembley Stadium is the venue for athletics, equestrianism, football, hockey and lacrosse as well as opening and closing ceremonies

1951   England beat Argentina 2-1 in the first official international at Wembley, other than against Scotland. The first 100,000 crowd, since 1923 Cup Final: Arsenal beat Liverpool 2-0.

1953	'The Matthews Cup Final': Blackpool beat Bolton 4-3 with Stanley Matthews starring for Blackpool and a hat-trick from Stan Mortensen. England's first loss at Wembley to a non-home nation, 6-3 to a Hungary side that included the legendary Ferenc Puskas
1955	Floodlights installed. First used for Inter-City Fairs Cup game between London and Frankfurt
1961	England beat Scotland 9-3 with Jimmy Greaves getting a hat-trick. Tottenham beat Leicester City 2-0 in FA Cup Final, to gain first league & cup double of 20th century
1963	Roof added and electronic scoreboard installed. Milan beat Benfica 2-1 in European Cup Final. Boxing: Henry Cooper loses to Cassius Clay in World Heavyweight Championship
1966	World Cup. Wembley hosts all England's games. England win the competition beating West Germany 4-2 (aet) in the final with Geoff Hurst scoring a hat-trick
1967	Third Division QPR beat West Bromwich Albion 3-2 in Wembley's first League Cup Final
1968	Manchester United beat Benfica 4-1 in European Cup Final. Royal International Horse Show held at stadium for first of two years
1971	Arsenal beat Liverpool 2-1 (aet) in the FA Cup Final, to win league & cup double. Ajax beat Panathinaikos 2-0 in European Cup Final
1972	West Germany beat England 3-1 in European Nations Cup Quarter-Final first leg (and win 3-1 on aggregate)
1975	Malcolm MacDonald scores all England's goals as they defeat Cyprus 5-0 in a Euro 76 qualifier. American Stunt motorcyclist Evel Knievel jumps 13 buses, but crash lands on down-slope receiving serious injuries
1977	After beating England in a Home International, Scottish fans invade the pitch and break the crossbars of each goal.
1978	Liverpool beat Bruges 1-0 in European Cup Final becoming the first British team to win the trophy twice
1981	Tottenham Hotspur beat Manchester City 3-2 in the first Wembley replay of an FA Cup Final
1982	Pope John Paul II holds mass at stadium. England defeat Luxembourg 9-0 in a Euro 84 qualifier
1985	Live Aid Concert held to raise money for African famine relief
1988	Computerised scoreboards installed. Concert for Nelson Mandela's 70th birthday (then in jail)
1990	Stadium becomes all-seater
1991	London Monarchs use Wembley as home venue in World League of American Football, winning the World Bowl
1992	Barcelona's 'Dream Team' beat Sampdoria 1-0 (aet) at Wembley's 5th European Cup Final
1995	Wigan win the Rugby League Challenge Cup for the eighth consecutive year, beating Leeds 30 points to 10. English Sports Council look into options for a new English National Stadium

1996   Euro 96 tournament. Wembley venue for all England games and the final. England lose on
        penalties in semi-finals to Germany who beat the Czech Republic 2-1 (aet) in the final.
        Wembley chosen as the site for the new English National Stadium after a bidding process

1999   Wembley National Stadium Ltd (a subsidiary of The FA) buy Wembley Stadium at a cost of
        £103m from Wembley plc. Manchester United defeat Newcastle United 2-0 in the FA Cup Final
        as part of their treble winning season

2000   Chelsea beat Aston Villa 1-0 in the last old Wembley FA Cup Final. Bon Jovi play the last concert.
        In the last football match of any kind, England lose 1-0 to Germany in a World Cup Qualifier.
        Preliminary demolition starts. The pitch is removed. Financing problems cause a two year delay.
        Pitch briefly replaced for filming of *Mike Bassett: England Manager*.

2002   Full demolition of stadium starts

2003   Twin Towers demolished. Construction of new stadium commences

2004   Raising of the arch and 'topping out' ceremony with Prime Minister Tony Blair and England
        captain David Beckham

2005   Construction continues but there are serious doubts over finishing on schedule. Multiplex
        announce probable losses of at least £70m on the project. Completion date slips from January
        2006 to end March 2006

2006   FA decide to switch FA Cup Final to Cardiff as new Wembley stadium won't be completed in
        time. Scheduled England friendlies are switched to other grounds too. Later it is announced
        that no matches will take place until 2007

2007   New Wembley completed. FA Cup Final, England games, Community Shield etc return, along
        with the Rugby League Challenge Cup Final. Muse headline first concerts at the new stadium.

2008   League Cup Final returns to Wembley

2012   Wembley to host finals of London Olympics football competitions

2018   FA considering bid to host 2018 World Cup, for which Wembley would be the centrepiece

Programme of the last football match staged at Wembley, England v. Germany, 7th October 2000

11

It wasn't only a draw at full time that could lead to 'extra time' at Wembley. If you were very keen and got to your Wembley match well in advance, you would be treated to an extensive programme of pre-match entertainment of up to two hours length! The programme from the 1976 England v. France Schoolboy International illustrates the excitement in store for the early arriving fan. The event was hosted by Ed 'Stewpot' Stewart, a popular BBC Radio One DJ of the time. First up was a twenty minute burst from the Romford Drum and Trumpet Corps. The Central Band of the Royal Air Force then took over for their twenty minutes of stardom, playing their interpretations of hits from such people as Simon and Garfunkel, The Beatles, The Seekers and even the dreaded 'Una Paloma Blanca', mixed in with more traditional favourites such as 'When the Saints Go Marching In'. 'You'll Never Walk Alone' also featured, along with 'Colonel Bogey', 'Circus Gallop' and the theme to 'The Dam Busters'. The Royal Air Force Dog Demonstration Team then showed what they were made of for another twenty minutes.

With the actual game still almost an hour away, at least there was then some football, in the shape of The Eurovision Penalty Prize competition. ITV Sport came up with the idea of the 'Penalty Prize' competition for the 1969-70 season. It was a regional weekly televised contest where selected schoolboys took five penalties each against professional goalkeepers. This culminated in a final which was played as part of the pre-match entertainment at the League Cup Final. The first took place in 1970, with Manchester United's Alex Stepney and Spurs' Pat Jennings facing penalties from regional winners from all over the UK. The concept proved popular and the competition spread around Europe, peaking in 1976 with The Eurovision Penalty Prize competition. Queens Park Rangers goalkeeper Phil Parkes faced a barrage of spot kicks from a host of teenagers, overseen by Britain's then best-known referee, Jack Taylor. Playing for the Gordon Banks Trophy were six 13 to 14 year old boys, from Denmark, England, Israel, the Netherlands, the Republic of Ireland and Turkey.

With half an hour still to fill before kick-off, Stewpot was back to lead 'Community Singing' for spectators, accompanied by an RAF band, to sing along to. This included contemporary hits such as 'Remember You're A Womble, 'Y Viva Espana', and 'Tie a Yellow Ribbon Round the Old Oak Tree'. After that, and presumably to everyone's relief, came the presentation of the teams and the National Anthems, a sure sign that real footie action is not far away!

It has long been commonplace for the National Anthems that are played before International matches to be sung along with, ignored, respected or booed. But there was an age in Britain when everyone stood to attention when the National Anthem was played in cinemas, let alone sporting events, and things were a little different. In 1940's Britain the National Anthem – God Save The King, as it was then - was actually played at the end of the match as opposed to the current tradition of before kick-off.

The hymn 'Abide With Me' has, over the years, become inextricably linked with football's FA Cup and Rugby League's Challenge Cup Final, being sung as part of the build up each year (bar one) since 1927. It was written in 1847 by Henry Lyte and is about the singers' heartfelt wish for God to be with them as the years pass and they approach death. It has nothing whatsoever to do with football though, and is said to have only been selected all those years ago through being a favourite of the then Queen Mary. It was kept as part of the Wembley build-up as it proved very popular with the fans. It was dropped at the 1975 FA Cup Final but was brought back immediately in 1976 by popular demand. In the early years the singing of 'Abide With Me' and the National Anthem were simply led by whoever was recruited to sing that year. In recent years, however, professional singers have been enlisted, which has not been to everyone's approval, and a petition was set up in 2006 asking for a return to the singing simply being led, rather than a 'pro' performing it whilst others listened.

The stadium is, of course, not the only major sporting or entertainment venue in Wembley. It's also not the only football venue in the area. And just to confuse matters, Wembley, Middlesex is not the only Wembley in the world! So, here are some of these 'other' Wembleys…

THE RAIL ROAD TO WEMBLEY

Although the standard of public transport to Wembley has often been criticised, there are three stations within easy walking distance of the stadium, with connections far and wide. Having suffered neglect in varying degrees over recent decades, all three have undergone a major makeover, if not total rebuild, for the new Wembley stadium.

Wembley Central: Bakerloo Line, Silverlink Metro (Euston – Watford Junction) & Southern (Watford Junction – Clapham Junction)

Other than for trains to take you out of the area, the tile-work featuring the stadium's twin towers was for many years the only redeeming feature of the very dismal Wembley Central Station. It opened in 1844 as 'Sudbury (for Wembley)', becoming 'Sudbury & Wembley' in 1882 and conversely, 'Wembley (for Sudbury)' in 1910. Fortunately the railway authorities finally got a grip on themselves and settled on the name 'Wembley Central' for the 1948 Olympics. Thankfully the station is receiving a thorough upgrade with an improved ticket office, more CCTV, lifts and a pedestrian footbridge, aiming to be able to handle up to 12,000 passengers an hour.

Wembley Stadium: Chiltern Railways (Marylebone – Aylesbury via Denham & Birmingham)

Closest to the stadium itself, Wembley Stadium, as it is now named, was first opened for passengers in 1906. It too has been through alternative names, starting life as 'Wembley Hill' and becoming 'Wembley Complex' in 1978. Having become rather overlooked and ignored, it will become much more of a focal point in the future. The battered old station building was finally demolished in 2006 to make way for the White Horse Bridge – part of the link from the High Street to the front of the stadium, and once complete, a new bus terminal will be directly outside.

Wembley Park: Metropolitan & Jubilee Lines, Chiltern Railways (Marylebone – Aylesbury)

Wembley Central Station

Opened in the 1894, Wembley Park Station is very much part of the Wembley story (see Chapter One). If you have the choice, it's probably the best station to arrive at, especially as you come out straight on to Olympic Way (aka Wembley Way) which has since 1948 led fans to the front of the stadium. This has also received a dramatic modernisation in order to cope with the hordes that descend on the town on match or gig days.

WEMBLEY ARENA

From Bowie to Busted, Steely Dan to The Spice Girls, ice-shows, pantomimes and Olympic swimming, Wembley Arena has hosted them all, and today finds itself as one of the top entertainment venues in the country. This famous neighbour of Wembley Stadium was built for the stadium's then owner Arthur Elvin in 1934, but for different purposes to those it is now best known for. Elvin's aim was simply to expand the range of sporting activities he could host, so, known originally as the Empire Pool & Sport Arena, his new venue was essentially a swimming venue with a 200 feet long pool. However, this could be converted to an ice-rink and, with the addition of flooring, also host many other indoor sports. A ceremonial laying of the foundation stone was carried out by the Earl of Derby in February 1934, with the building formally opened by the Duke of Gloucester in July of that year. The opening event was a diving display by the Highgate Diving Club followed by a banquet for one thousand invited guests. A popular Elvin-inspired feature was the rink-side restaurant allowing the sophistication of a meal while enjoying the sporting activity or other entertainment.

In its early years the Empire Pool hosted swimming events for the Empire Games and European Championships. Overall though it wasn't a success and after the 1948 Olympics it was never used for swimming again. Elvin and his team were always looking to try out new things but probably the oddest experiment of all was 'Tennice' – an amusing mix of tennis and ice-skating, which was tried in 1940 – but just the once. In subsequent years, and with much greater success, it became a venue for tennis, table tennis, figure-skating, indoor speed-

Wembley Arena

way, boxing, basketball and athletics. From the 1950s onwards it further diversified to host popular ice-shows, ice-hockey (as home venue for Wembley Lions and Wembley Canadians), show jumping, cycling and best known of all, countless rock and pop concerts – becoming a near essential stop on any major band or artist's tour schedule with its capacity of 10,000. A highlight of one of the 1950's ice shows was the bizarre appearance on the ice of a Comet aircraft. The world-famous Harlem Globetrotters basketball team also played there during their world tours in the 1970s and 1980s.

A few weeks after John Lennon's infamous quote that The Beatles were 'more popular than Jesus now', on May Day 1966 the 'Fab Four' performed their last ever UK gig, at the Empire Pool, at the New Musical Express Poll Winners concert with a five song, 15 minute set. Other artists included Herman's Hermits, Roy Orbison, Cliff Richard, The Rolling Stones, The Seekers, The Shadows, The Small Faces, Dusty Springfield, The Walker Brothers, The Who and The Yardbirds. In November

Wembley FC

1974 Pink Floyd performed their ground breaking and record breaking album, *'The Dark Side of the Moon'* in its entirety there.

Five-A-Side Football first took off during World War Two with tournaments for all the London sides at various other venues around the capital. After these petered out, it was revived at the Empire Pool in 1967, with West Ham United coming out on top. The format was usually sixteen teams in a knockout competition, with the whole tournament staged on the one night. Queens Park Rangers proved particularly successful, winning four times between 1971 and 1980, whilst in 1994 lowly Wycombe Wanderers, though not strictly a London team, were surprise winners. The footballing world beyond the capital also wanted to get involved and the Daily Express sponsored a national competition held at what was now called Wembley Arena. Charlton Athletic won the first in 1968. Other notable winners included Wolverhampton Wanderers, in 1975 and 1976 and Celtic in 1981.

Now under different ownership to the stadium, Wembley Arena, as it became known in 1976, con-tinues as strongly as ever, reopening in 2006 after a £35m refurbishment, with its main entrance switched to the stadium end.

WEMBLEY CONFERENCE CENTRE

Completing the trio of neighbouring venues is the Conference Centre, opened in January 1977 as the country's first purpose built conference venue. It has hosted such varied events as the 1977 Eurovision Song Contest, a 1980 Thames TV Telethon with Rolf Harris, the British Beauty Championships, Dog Shows and for several years in the 1980s, the BAFTA Awards Ceremony. Perhaps best known of all was snooker's annual showpiece Masters Tournament, which took place there from 1979 to 2006, with audiences of up to 2,800 watching the likes of Alex Higgins, Ray Reardon, Jimmy White, Steve Davis, Stephen Hendry and Ronnie O'Sullivan showing their skills on the green baize. It has also been a regular boxing venue. But away from the more glamorous events its bread and butter has, not surprisingly, been earned through hosting conferences, along with exhibitions, banquets and University award ceremonies.

The Snooker Masters has already sought green-baize pastures elsewhere, at Wembley Arena, and as part of the major redevelopment of the surrounding area, the Conference Centre will be demolished.

WEMBLEY FC

Not to be confused with the larger stadium a couple of miles north, Vale Farm, Sudbury is the home of non-league Wembley FC, which has a capacity of 2,000. 'The Lions', who are to be found much lower down in football's pecking order than the teams who generally play at the national stadium, are currently in the Combined Counties League Premier Division. They were formed in 1946 and these days attract crowds of a few hundred at best. They did actually make one appearance at 'the other Wembley', losing 2-0 to Hendon in the 1988 Final of the Middlesex Charity Cup. Their other association with their better-known namesake is that the England World Cup winning squad of '66 trained there prior to winning the tournament.

Wasps Rugby Union Club used to be a neighbour but moved away in the 1990s, their ground now the site of a housing association development.

WEMBLEY v. OTHER MAJOR STADIA

In this age of modern, sophisticated and thankfully much more safety and comfort conscious stadia, the old records are just not going to be broken. Wembley's highest attendance of over 200,000 was for its first ever event, back in 1923, and will never be topped. In any case, this is an unofficial figure – the official attendance being recorded as 126,047 – representing those that paid.

The Mario Filho Stadium in Rio De Janeiro, Brazil – better known as 'The Maracana' holds the official world record attendance of 199,854. This was for the 1950 World Cup Final to see Uruguay beat Brazil 2-1. It was described as the biggest building site in the world at the time, and wasn't actually finished until 1965. It is owned by the City authorities and is the home ground for four Rio based clubs. Its capacity is now 120,000. Until the Maracana was built the attendance record had been held by Hampden Park in Glasgow (home to Queens Park FC and the Scottish national team) with 149,547 witnessing a Scottish 3-1 victory over England in April 1937.

Of the best-known stadia around Europe, Berlin's Olympiastadion, which hosted the final and five other games in the 2006 World Cup, now has a capacity of 74,400 after modernisation, although this was reduced to 66,000 for safety reasons in the World Cup. Originally built for the 1936 Olympics, it is home to club side Hertha Berlin. Real Madrid's Bernabeu has a capacity of 105,000, Barcelona's Camp Nou is 93,000 (plans to make it 150,000 were abandoned), the Stade De France in Paris where the World Cup Final of 1998 was held comes in at 80,000, and the San Siro in Milan, Italy (home of Milan and Internazionale) was expanded to 83,000 for the 1990 World Cup.

In the UK, while Wembley has been out of action the stadia that have largely taken the strain have been Cardiff's Millennium Stadium, which opened in 1999 with a capacity of 74,500, and Manchester United's Old Trafford, recently expanded to 76,000.

The Mario Filho Stadium in Rio De Janeiro, Brazil – better known as 'The Maracana'

WEMBLEY ALL OVER THE WORLD

Probably the furthest 'other' Wembley from Wembley is the one five kilometres north-west of Perth, the capital of Western Australia. Sitting half-way between the city, City Beach and Scarborough Beach, it has good access to the local freeways and major roads, and the area has many pleasant tree lined avenues and well established gardens. It was back in 1924 that Perth City Council decided that the area would be named Wembley Park, after the suburb of Greater London where the Empire Exhibition was then being held. Over the years however, it has been shortened to just plain 'Wembley'.

The State of Alberta in Canada has its own town of Wembley, not far from the city of Grand Prairie, while surprisingly the USA only manages a Wembley Shopping Centre in Tulsa, Oklahoma. South Africa has two towns called Wembley, one being in Pietermaritzburg, KwaZulu-Natal; the other in Johannesburg which featured the Union Ice-Rink at Turffontein Road, home to that nation's own Wembley Lions ice-hockey team until 1975. There is also a Wembley Square – a modern apartment block in Wembley Street in a suburb of Cape Town called Gardens.

The thrill and spills of the FA Cup were reproduced in the 'WEMBLEY' board game. The early 1970s edition is shown here, but the game was first available in the late 1940s, produced by Ariel Productions Ltd.

WEMBLEY FOR KIDS

WEMBLEY BOARD GAME

The thrill and spills of the FA Cup were reproduced in the 'WEMBLEY' board game. The game was first available in the late 1940s, produced by Ariel Productions Ltd. The pleasures of football recreated through dice, cards and plastic tokens would probably be lost on the computer games' generation but in its heyday it was deemed good enough for the accompanying booklet to proclaim that 'so skilfully is the game of Wembley designed that the thrills, the fever and the surprises of the actual Cup competition are faithfully reflected in the play…'.

SUBBUTEO WEMBLEY ROYAL BOX

In the early 1970s Subbuteo were manufacturers of the monumentally popular table football game, along with the rugby, cricket and hockey versions. They brought out an accessory in their ever expanding range; the Royal Box at Wembley. This consisted of 00 scale figures set into a green, black and white cardboard box, which simulated the famous 39 steps and the Royal Box itself. The figures were a red coated, yellow hatted Queen Elizabeth II holding the FA Cup in her hands, plus various other dignitaries. Many a simulated Wembley lap of honour was postponed due to the inability of an 00 scale captain to wrest the trophy from Her Majesty's tight grip.

LEGO WEMBLEY

The Miniland section of Legoland at Windsor recreates many famous landmarks around the world, so naturally a Lego reproduction of Wembley Stadium is to be found there. Both the old stadium and the new have been featured, including a Lego streaker racing across the pitch at full time for a football final at the old stadium; itself another Wembley first!

Thanks to Arthur Elvin, Wembley got beyond its first handful of games and went on to host over 750 matches from 28th April 1923 to 7th October 2000. We have summarised some aspects of this.

Type of match	No.
England (official) internationals	223
England unofficial internationals	10
Other Full Internationals	4
Other unofficial internationals	1
Amateur Internationals	5
FA Cup Finals	72
FA Cup Final Replays	5
FA Cup Semi-Finals	7
League Cup Finals	34
FA Charity Shields	27
Full Members Cup Finals	7
Football League Trophy Finals	16
League Promotion Play-Off Finals	33
Other club matches	23
European Cup Finals	5
European Cup Winners Cup Finals	2
Other European Club Competition	11
FA Amateur Cup Finals	26
FA Trophy Finals	31
FA Vase Finals	26
Varsity Matches	38
Other non-league club matches	26
Women's/Girls Matches	3
Schoolboy/Youth/U18/U23 matches	105
Other representative matches	3
Olympic Games/Qualifiers	6

Most FA Cup Final wins at Wembley

Manchester United	8
Arsenal	7
Tottenham Hotspur	7
Newcastle United	5
Liverpool	5

Most FA Cup Final Appearances at Wembley

Arsenal	14
Manchester United	13
Liverpool	10
Tottenham Hotspur	8
Newcastle United	8
Everton	8

Most Football League Cup Final wins at Wembley (1967-2000):

Liverpool (one at a replay)	5
Aston Villa	4
Nottingham Forest	4

Most FA Amateur Cup Final wins at Wembley (1949-74):

Crook Town	4
Bishop Auckland	3
Hendon	3

Most FA Trophy Final wins at Wembley (1970-2000):

Scarborough	3
Telford United	3
Woking	3

Most FA Vase Final wins at Wembley (1975-2000):

Billericay Town	3
Bridlington Town	2
Halesowen Town	2
Tiverton Town	2

Club sides with the most Wembley appearances:

Arsenal	41
Cambridge University	38
Oxford University	36
Manchester United	32
Liverpool	26

Non-English Club sides with the most Wembley appearances:

Milan (Italy)	3
Sampdoria (Italy)	3
Dynamo Kiev (Ukraine)	3

Most frequently occurring Wembley fixtures:

Oxford v. Cambridge	36
England v. Scotland	30
England v. Scotland (Schoolboy)	21
England v. Northern Ireland	18
England v. Wales	16

The fastest goal at Wembley was scored by Maurice Cox of Cambridge University after just 20 seconds against Oxford University on 5th December 1979.

The fastest goal in a full international was by Bryan Robson in 38 seconds for England vs Yugoslavia on 13th December 1989.

England Internationals

England played 223 official matches at Wembley against 49 different opponents (counting Germany & West Germany together and Czechoslovakia & Czech Republic together). Over a quarter of these games were against other 'home' nations, with the most frequent opponent being Scotland.   Wembley internationals against non-home nations didn't commence until 1951 but with the ending of the Home International Championships in 1984, matches against Scotland, Wales and Northern Ireland have become rarer while friendlies against other nations have increased. From these games, England's biggest margin of victory was 9-0 over Luxembourg in 1982, while their biggest margin of defeat was 5-1 against Scotland in 1928. Most goals conceded was in the 6-3 defeat by Hungary in 1953.

England's record against opponents played 4 times or more at Wembley

OPPONENT	Plyd	W	D	L	F	A
Scotland	30	16	5	9	68	41
N. Ireland	18	13	3	2	42	12
Wales	16	10	5	1	37	14
Brazil	9	2	5	2	11	11
Germany/W.Germany	9	4	0	5	13	11
Hungary	7	6	0	1	15	7
Portugal	7	5	2	0	11	3
Argentina	6	3	3	0	10	6
Poland	6	5	1	0	14	3
Spain	6	5	0	1	12	4
Switzerland	6	3	3	0	10	5
Netherlands	6	2	3	1	10	7
Yugoslavia	6	4	2	0	13	5
France	5	4	0	1	13	2
Denmark	5	4	0	1	4	1
Italy	5	2	2	1	5	3
Rep. of Ireland	5	3	2	0	11	4
Czechoslovakia/Czech R.	5	4	1	0	10	2
Austria	4	2	1	1	14	6
Bulgaria	4	2	2	0	4	1
Romania	4	0	4	0	3	3
Turkey	4	4	0	0	18	0
Uruguay	4	1	2	1	3	3
USSR	4	2	1	1	10	5
Sweden	4	1	2	1	5	4

** Data has been compiled from a wide variety of sources as listed in acknowledgements. Estimated dates have been used for some minor games where the actual date could not be verified.*

28/04/23	Bolton Wanderers v. West Ham United	2-0	F.A. Cup Final
12/04/24	England v. Scotland	1-1	Home International
26/04/24	Newcastle United v. Aston Villa	2-0	F.A. Cup Final
25/04/25	Sheffield United v. Cardiff City	1-0	F.A. Cup Final
24/04/26	Bolton Wanderers v. Manchester City	1-0	F.A. Cup Final
23/04/27	Cardiff City v. Arsenal	1-0	F.A. Cup Final
31/03/28	England v. Scotland	1-5	Home International
21/04/28	Blackburn Rovers v. Huddersfield Town	3-1	F.A. Cup Final
30/09/28	Ealing Association v. Hastings & St Leonards	1-0	Southern Amateur League
13/10/28	Ealing Association v. Ipswich Town	0-4	Southern Amateur League
20/10/28	Ealing Association v. Midland Bank	0-4	Southern Amateur League
27/10/28	Ealing Association v. Bank Of England	1-5	Southern Amateur League
03/11/28	Ealing Association v. Westminster Bank	0-3	Southern Amateur League
17/11/28	Cambridge University v. The Casuals	5-2	Friendly
24/11/28	Ealing Association v. Aquarius	0-3	Southern Amateur League
01/12/28	Ealing Association v. Old Lyonians	0-3	Southern Amateur League
14/01/29	Barclays Bank v. Old Malvernians	2-1	Arthur Dunn Cup
21/01/29	Cambridge University v. London University	3-0	Varsity Match
28/01/29	Old Malvernians v. Old Cholmeleians	4-2	Arthur Dunn Cup
04/02/29	London v. Middlesex	5-1	Schoolboy Charity Match
27/04/29	Bolton Wanderers v. Portsmouth	2-0	F.A. Cup Final
22/02/30	Harrow St.Marys v. Glacier Sports	5-4 (aet)	Wembley Hospital Cup Final
05/04/30	England v. Scotland	5-2	Home International
26/04/30	Arsenal v. Huddersfield Town	2-0	F.A. Cup Final
22/11/30	Clapton Orient v. Brentford	3-0	Division 3 (South)
06/12/30	Clapton Orient v. Southend United	3-1	Division 3 (South)
25/04/31	West Bromwich Alb. v. Birmingham Cty	2-1	F.A. Cup Final
09/04/32	England v. Scotland	3-0	Home International
23/04/32	Newcastle United v. Arsenal	2-1	F.A. Cup Final
29/04/33	Everton v. Manchester City	3-0	F.A. Cup Final
07/04/34	Walthamstow Fellowship v.Greenwich Traf.	1-0	London Occupational League
14/04/34	England v. Scotland	3-0	Home International
28/04/34	Manchester City v. Portsmouth	2-1	F.A. Cup Final
27/04/35	Sheffield Wednesday v. West Bromwich	4-2	F.A. Cup Final
04/04/36	England v. Scotland	1-1	Home International
25/04/36	Arsenal v. Sheffield United	1-0	F.A. Cup Final
01/04/37	GB University XI v. German University	1-0	Friendly
01/05/37	Sunderland v. Preston North End	3-1	F.A. Cup Final
09/04/38	England v. Scotland	0-1	Home International
30/04/38	Preston North End v. Huddersfield Town	1-0 (aet)	F.A. Cup Final
29/04/39	Portsmouth v. Wolverhampton Wanderers	4-1	F.A. Cup Final
13/04/40	England v. Wales	0-1	Unofficial Wartime International
08/06/40	West Ham United v. Blackburn Rovers	1-0	Football League War Cup
08/04/41	RAF v. Metropolitan Police	6-3	Charity Match
10/05/41	Arsenal v. Preston North End	1-1	Football League War Cup
04/10/41	England v. Scotland	2-0	Unofficial Wartime International
03/11/41	Belgium v. Netherlands	5-4	Unofficial Wartime International
17/01/42	England v. Scotland	3-0	Unofficial Wartime International
01/05/42	Brentford v. Portsmouth	2-0	London War Cup Final
03/06/42	Wealdstone v. RAF Uxbridge	5-2 (aet)	Mddx Senior Red Cross Cup Final
10/10/42	England v. Scotland	0-0	Unofficial Wartime International
27/02/43	England v. Wales	5-3	Unofficial Wartime International
06/05/43	Arsenal v. Charlton Athletic	7-1	Football League South Cup
29/05/43	England v. Wales	8-3	Unofficial Wartime International
01/06/43	RAF v. Metropolitan Police	4-3	Charity Match
02/06/43	Finchley v. Southall	1-0	Mddx Senior Red Cross Cup Final
19/02/44	England v. Scotland	6-2	Unofficial Wartime Inter
15/04/44	Charlton Athletic v. Chelsea	3-1	Football League South Cup
08/05/44	Combined Services v. Metropolitan Police	5-2	Charity Match
01/06/44	Tufnell Park v. Queens Park Rangers Juniors	3-2	Mddx Senior Red Cross Cup Final
14/10/44	England v. Scotland	6-2	Unofficial Wartime International
04/04/45	Chelsea v. Millwall	2-0	Football League South Cup
08/05/45	Combined Services v. National Police	3-1	Charity Match
24/05/45	Golders Green v. Tufnell Park	4-1	Mddx Senior Red Cross Cup Final

26/05/45	England v. France	2-2	Victory International (unofficial)
19/01/46	England v. Belgium	2-0	Victory International (unofficial)
20/04/46	Air Training Corps v. N.A. Of Boys Clubs	4-2	British Junior Cup Final
20/04/46	Army Physical Training Corps XI v. F.A. XI	5-3	International Trial
27/04/46	Derby County v. Charlton Athletic	4-1 (aet)	F.A. Cup Final
12/04/47	England v. Scotland	1-1	Home International
26/04/47	Charlton Athletic v. Burnley	1-0 (aet)	F.A. Cup Final
24/04/48	Air Training Corps v. Army Cadet Force	2-0	British Junior Cup Final
24/04/48	Manchester United v. Blackpool	4-2	F.A. Cup Final
10/08/48	Sweden v. Denmark	4-2	Olympic Games Semi-Final
11/08/48	Yugoslavia v. Great Britain	3-1	Olympic Games Semi-Final
13/08/48	Sweden v. Yugoslavia	3-1	Olympic Games Final
13/08/48	Denmark v. Great Britain	5-3	Olympic Games Bronze Medal
09/04/49	Air Training Corps v. N.A. Of Boys Clubs	2-2 (aet)	British Junior Cup Final
09/04/49	England v. Scotland	1-3	Home International
23/04/49	Bromley v. Romford	1-0	F.A. Amateur Cup Final
30/04/49	Wolverhampton Wanderers v. Leicester City	3-1	F.A. Cup Final
22/04/50	England v. Scotland	8-2	Schoolboy International
22/04/50	Willmington v. Bishop Auckland	4-0	F.A. Amateur Cup Final
29/04/50	Arsenal v. Liverpool	2-1	F.A. Cup Final
13/05/50	N.A. Of Boys Clubs v. Army Cadet Force	4-1	British Junior Cup Final
13/05/50	Essex v. Middlesex	2-1 (aet)	FA County Yth Cup Final
13/04/51	England v. Wales	3-0	Schoolboy International
14/04/51	England v. Scotland	2-3	Home International
21/04/51	Pegasus v. Bishop Auckland	2-1	F.A. Amateur Cup Final
28/04/51	Newcastle United v. Blackpool	2-0	F.A. Cup Final
09/05/51	N.A. Of Boys Clubs v. Army Cadet Force	4-2	British Junior Cup Final
09/05/51	England v. Argentina	2-1	Friendly
28/11/51	England v. Austria	2-2	Friendly
15/03/52	England v. Scotland	1-2	Amateur International
05/04/52	England v. Scotland	1-0	Schoolboy International
26/04/52	Walthamstow Avenue v. Leyton	2-1	F.A. Amateur Cup Final
03/05/52	Newcastle United v. Arsenal	1-0	F.A. Cup Final
10/05/52	N.A. Of Boys Clubs v. Air Training Corps	5-3	British Junior Cup Final
12/11/52	England v. Wales	5-2	Home International
26/11/52	England v. Belgium	5-0	Friendly
06/12/52	Cambridge University v. Oxford University	1-2	Varsity Match
07/01/53	Cambridge University v. Oxford University	0-0	Varsity Match
28/03/53	England v. Wales	3-3	Schoolboy International
11/04/53	Pegasus v. Harwich & Parkeston	6-0	F.A. Amateur Cup Final
18/04/53	England v. Scotland	2-2	Home International
02/05/53	Blackpool v. Bolton Wanderers	4-3	F.A. Cup Final
09/05/53	N.A. Of Boys Clubs v. Air Training Corps	3-1	British Junior Cup Final
21/10/53	England v. Rest of Europe XI	4-4	Friendly
25/11/53	England v. Hungary	3-6	Friendly
05/12/53	Cambridge University v. Oxford University	1-1	Varsity Match
27/03/54	England v. Scotland	1-4	British Amateur Championship
03/04/54	England v. Scotland	1-0	Schoolboy International
10/04/54	Crook Town v. Bishop Auckland	2-2 (aet)	F.A. Amateur Cup Final
01/05/54	West Bromwich Albion v. Preston North End	3-2	F.A. Cup Final
08/05/54	Air Training Corps v. N.A. Of Boys Clubs	1-0	British Junior Cup Final
10/11/54	England v. Wales	3-2	Home International
01/12/54	England v. West Germany	3-1	Friendly
04/12/54	Cambridge University v. Oxford University	3-2	Varsity Match
02/04/55	England v. Scotland	7-2	Home International
16/04/55	Bishop Auckland v. Hendon	2-0	F.A. Amateur Cup Final
23/04/55	England v. Wales	6-0	Schoolboy International
07/05/55	Newcastle United v. Manchester City	3-1	F.A. Cup Final
26/10/55	London v. Frankfurt (West Germany)	3-2	Inter-Cities Fairs Cup (Group)
02/11/55	England v. Northern Ireland	3-0	Home International
30/11/55	England v. Spain	4-1	Friendly
07/12/55	Cambridge University v. Oxford University	4-2	Varsity Match
24/03/56	England v. Scotland	4-2	British Amateur Championship
07/04/56	Bishop Auckland v. Corinthians	1-1 (aet)	F.A. Amateur Cup Final
21/04/56	England v. Scotland	1-2	Schoolboy International
05/05/56	Manchester City v. Birmingham City	3-1	F.A. Cup Final
09/05/56	England v. Brazil	4-2	Friendly
12/05/56	N.A. Of Boys Clubs v. Army Cadet Force	2-1	British Junior Cup Final
12/05/56	Great Britain v. Bulgaria	3-3	Olympic Qualifier 2nd leg

Date	Match	Score	Type
14/11/56	England v. Wales	3-1	Home International
28/11/56	England v. Yugoslavia	3-0	Friendly
08/12/56	Oxford University v. Cambridge University	4-1	Varsity Match
30/03/57	England v. Wales	2-0	Schoolboy International
06/04/57	England v. Scotland	2-1	Home International
13/04/57	Bishop Auckland v. Wycombe Wanderers	3-1	F.A. Amateur Cup Final
04/05/57	Aston Villa v. Manchester United	2-1	F.A. Cup Final
08/05/57	England v. Republic Of Ireland	5-1	World Cup Qualifier
16/10/57	England v. Romania	3-2	Under 23 International
06/11/57	England v. Northern Ireland	2-3	Home International
27/11/57	England v. France	4-0	Friendly
07/12/57	Cambridge University v. Oxford University	1-1	Varsity Match
29/03/58	England v. Scotland	2-3	British Amateur Championship
12/04/58	Woking v. Ilford	3-0	F.A. Amateur Cup Final
26/04/58	England v. Scotland	3-1	Schoolboy International
03/05/58	Bolton Wanderers v. Manchester United	2-0	F.A. Cup Final
07/05/58	England v. Portugal	2-1	Friendly
22/10/58	England v. USSR	5-0	Friendly
06/12/58	Cambridge University v. Oxford University	1-1	Varsity Match
11/04/59	England v. Scotland	1-0	Home International
18/04/59	Crook Town v. Barnet	3-2	F.A. Amateur Cup Final
25/04/59	England v. West Germany	2-0	Schoolboy International
02/05/59	Nottingham Forest v. Luton Town	2-1	F.A. Cup Final
06/05/59	England v. Italy	2-2	Friendly
28/10/59	England v. Sweden	2-3	Friendly
18/11/59	England v. Northern Ireland	2-1	Home International
03/12/59	Cambridge University v. Oxford University	6-2	Varsity Match
23/04/60	Hendon v. Kingstonian	2-1	F.A. Amateur Cup Final
30/04/60	England v. Scotland	5-3	Schoolboy International
07/05/60	Wolverhampton Wanderers v. Blackburn	3-0	F.A. Cup Final
11/05/60	England v. Yugoslavia	3-3	Friendly
26/10/60	England v. Spain	4-2	Friendly
23/11/60	England v. Wales	5-1	Home International
07/12/60	Cambridge University v. Oxford University	2-2	Varsity Match
15/04/61	England v. Scotland	9-3	Home International
22/04/61	Walthamstowe Avenue v. West Auckland	2-1	F.A. Amateur Cup Final
29/04/61	England v. Wales	8-1	Schoolboy International
06/05/61	Tottenham Hotspur v. Leicester City	2-0	F.A. Cup Final
10/05/61	England v. Mexico	8-0	Friendly
25/10/61	England v. Portugal	2-0	World Cup Qualifier
22/11/61	England v. Northern Ireland	1-1	Home International
09/12/61	Cambridge University v. Oxford University	2-0	Varsity Match
04/04/62	England v. Austria	3-1	Friendly
21/04/62	Crook Town v. Hounslow Town	1-1 (aet)	F.A. Amateur Cup Final
28/04/62	England v. West Germany	1-3	Schoolboy International
05/05/62	Tottenham Hotspur v. Burnley	3-1	F.A. Cup Final
09/05/62	England v. Switzerland	3-1	Friendly
21/11/62	England v. Wales	4-0	Home International
08/12/62	Cambridge University v. Oxford University	5-2	Varsity Match
06/04/63	England v. Scotland	1-2	Home International
23/04/63	England v. Northern Ireland	4-0	European Youth Tournament
27/04/63	England v. Wales	4-1	Schoolboy International
04/05/63	Wimbledon v. Sutton United	4-2	F.A. Amateur Cup Final
06/05/63	England v. Uruguay	2-1	Friendly
08/05/63	England v. Brazil	1-1	Friendly
22/05/63	Milan (Italy) v. Benfica (Portugal)	2-1	European Cup Final
25/05/63	Manchester United v. Leicester City	3-1	F.A. Cup Final
23/10/63	England v. Rest Of The World XI	2-1	Friendly
06/11/63	England v. Rest Of The UK XI	5-2	U18 Youth International
20/11/63	England v. Northern Ireland	8-3	Home International
07/12/63	Cambridge University v. Oxford University	4-2	Varsity Match
18/04/64	Crook Town v. Enfield Town	2-1	F.A. Amateur Cup Final
25/04/64	England v. West Germany	1-1	Schoolboy International
02/05/64	West Ham United v. Preston North End	3-2	F.A. Cup Final
21/10/64	England v. Belgium	2-2	Friendly
18/11/64	England v. Wales	2-1	Home International
05/12/64	Cambridge University v. Oxford University	3-1	Varsity Match
03/04/65	England v. Scotland	3-0	Schoolboy International
10/04/65	England v. Scotland	2-2	Home International

24/04/65	Hendon v. Whitby Town	3-1	F.A. Amateur Cup Final
01/05/65	Liverpool v. Leeds United	2-1 (aet)	F.A. Cup Final
05/05/65	England v. Hungary	1-0	Friendly
19/05/65	West Ham United v. TSV Munchen 1860	2-0	European Cup Winners Cup
20/10/65	England v. Austria	2-3	Friendly
10/11/65	England v. Northern Ireland	2-1	Home International
08/12/65	Cambridge University v. Oxford University	3-2	Varsity Match
23/02/66	England v. West Germany	1-0	Friendly
16/04/66	Wealdstone v. Hendon	3-1	F.A. Amateur Cup Final
30/04/66	England v. West Germany	2-1	Schoolboy International
04/05/66	England v. Yugoslavia	2-0	Friendly
14/05/66	Everton v. Sheffield Wednesday	3-2	F.A. Cup Final
11/07/66	England v. Uruguay	0-0	World Cup Group Match
13/07/66	France v. Mexico	1-1	World Cup Group Match
15/07/66	Uruguay v. France	2-1	World Cup Group Match
16/07/66	England v. Mexico	2-0	World Cup Group Match
20/07/66	England v. France	2-0	World Cup Group Match
23/07/66	England v. Argentina	1-0	World Cup Qtr-Final
26/07/66	England v. Portugal	2-1	World Cup Semi-Final
28/07/66	Portugal v. USSR	4-2 (aet)	World Cup 3rd Place Match
30/07/66	England v. West Germany	4-2 (aet)	World Cup Final
02/11/66	England v. Czechoslovakia	0-0	Friendly
16/11/66	England v. Wales	5-1	Euro Qualifier/Home Inter.
07/12/66	Cambridge University v. Oxford University	1-0	Varsity Match
04/03/67	Queens Park Rangers v. West Bromwich	3-2	League Cup Final
15/04/67	England v. Scotland	2-3	Euro Qualifier/Home Inter.
22/04/67	Enfield Town v. Skelmersdale United	0-0 (aet)	F.A. Amateur Cup Final
29/04/67	England v. Scotland	0-2	Schoolboy International
20/05/67	Tottenham Hotspur v. Chelsea	2-1	F.A. Cup Final
24/05/67	England v. Spain	2-0	Friendly
22/11/67	England v. Northern Ireland	2-0	Euro Qualifier/Home Inter.
06/12/67	England v. USSR	2-2	Friendly
13/12/67	Cambridge University v. Oxford University	1-0	Varsity Match
02/03/68	Leeds United v. Arsenal	1-0	League Cup Final
03/04/68	England v. Spain	1-0	Friendly
20/04/68	Leytonstone v. Chesham United	1-0	F.A. Amateur Cup Final
27/04/68	England v. West Germany	1-2	Schoolboy International
18/05/68	West Bromwich Albion v. Everton	1-0 (aet)	F.A. Cup Final
22/05/68	England v. Sweden	3-1	Friendly
29/05/68	Manchester United v. Benfica (Portugal)	4-1 (aet)	European Cup Final
04/12/68	Cambridge University v. Oxford University	3-1	Varsity Match
11/12/68	England v. Bulgaria	1-1	Friendly
15/01/69	England v. Romania	1-1	Friendly
12/03/69	England v. France	5-0	Friendly
15/03/69	Swindon Town v. Arsenal	3-1 (aet)	League Cup Final
12/04/69	North Shields v. Sutton United	2-1	F.A. Amateur Cup Final
19/04/69	England v. Wales	3-0	Schoolboy International
26/04/69	Manchester City v. Leicester City	1-0	F.A. Cup Final
07/05/69	England v. Wales	2-1	Home International
10/05/69	England v. Scotland	4-1	Home International
03/12/69	Cambridge University v. Oxford University	1-1	Varsity Match
10/12/69	England v. Portugal	1-0	Friendly
14/01/70	England v. The Netherlands	0-0	Friendly
07/03/70	Manchester City v. West Bromwich Albion	2-1 (aet)	League Cup Final
21/03/70	England v. Scotland	2-0	Schoolboy International
04/04/70	Enfield Town v. Dagenham	5-1	F.A. Amateur Cup Final
11/04/70	Chelsea v. Leeds United	2-2 (aet)	F.A. Cup Final
21/04/70	England v. Northern Ireland	3-1	Home International
02/05/70	Macclesfield Town v. Telford United	2-0	F.A. Trophy Final
16/05/70	England v. West Germany	3-0	Schoolboy International
25/11/70	England v. East Germany	3-1	Friendly
09/12/70	Cambridge University v. Oxford University	1-0	Varsity Match
27/02/71	Tottenham Hotspur v. Aston Villa	2-0	League Cup Final
21/03/71	England v. Northern Ireland	1-0	Schoolboy International
24/03/71	Great Britain v. Bulgaria	1-0	Olympic Qualifier 1st leg
03/04/71	England v. The Netherlands	5-1	Schoolboy International
21/04/71	England v. Greece	3-0	Euro. Nations Cup (Group)
24/04/71	Skelmersdale United v. Dagenham	4-1	F.A. Amateur Cup Final
01/05/71	Telford United v. Hillingdon Borough	3-2	F.A. Trophy Final

08/05/71	Arsenal v. Liverpool	2-1 (aet)	F.A. Cup Final
12/05/71	England v. Malta	5-0	Euro. Nations Cup (Group)
19/05/71	England v. Wales	0-0	Home International
22/05/71	England v. Scotland	3-1	Home International
20/06/71	Ajax (Netherlands) v. Panathinaikos (Greece)	2-0	European Cup Final
10/11/71	England v. Switzerland	1-1	Euro. Nations Cup (Group)
08/12/71	Cambridge University v. Oxford University	0-0	Varsity Match
04/03/72	Stoke City v. Chelsea	2-1	League Cup Final
15/04/72	Stafford Rangers v. Barnet	3-0	F.A. Trophy Final
22/04/72	Hendon v. Enfield Town	2-0	F.A. Amateur Cup Final
29/04/72	England v. West Germany	1-3	Euro. Nations Cup Q-Final
06/05/72	Leeds United v. Arsenal	1-0	F.A. Cup Final
20/05/72	England v. West Germany	4-0	Schoolboy International
23/05/72	England v. Northern Ireland	0-1	Home International
11/10/72	England v. Yugoslavia	1-1	Friendly
06/12/72	Cambridge University v. Oxford University	2-1	Varsity Match
03/01/73	The Three v. The Six	2-0	EEC Celebration Match
24/01/73	England v. Wales	1-1	World Cup Qualifier
03/03/73	Tottenham Hotspur v. Norwich City	1-0	League Cup Final
07/04/73	England v. The Netherlands	3-1	Schoolboy International
14/04/73	Walton & Hersham v. Slough Town	1-0	F.A. Amateur Cup Final
28/04/73	Scarborough v. Wigan Athletic	2-1	F.A. Trophy Final
05/05/73	Sunderland v. Leeds United	1-0	F.A. Cup Final
15/05/73	England v. Wales	3-0	Home International
19/05/73	England v. Scotland	1-0	Home International
09/06/73	England v. Scotland	2-4	Schoolboy International
26/09/73	England v. Austria	7-0	Friendly
17/10/73	England v. Poland	1-1	World Cup Qualifier
31/10/73	England v. West Germany	1-0	European Amateur C'ship
14/11/73	England v. Italy	0-1	Friendly
05/12/73	Cambridge University v. Oxford University	0-0	Varsity Match
02/03/74	Wolverhampton Wanderers v. Manchester United	2-1	League Cup Final
06/04/74	England v. France	5-2	Schoolboy International
20/04/74	Bishops Stortford v. Ilford	4-1	F.A. Amateur Cup Final
27/04/74	Morecambe v. Dartford	2-1	F.A. Trophy Final
04/05/74	Liverpool v. Newcastle United	3-0	F.A. Cup Final
15/05/74	England v. Northern Ireland	1-0	Home International
22/05/74	England v. Argentina	2-2	Friendly
01/06/74	England v. West Germany	4-0	Schoolboy International
09/06/74	Plymouth v. Sheffield	3-1	N.A. of Youth Clubs Cup
10/08/74	Liverpool v. Leeds United	0-0 (6-5pen)	F.A. Charity Shield
30/10/74	England v. Czechoslovakia	3-0	Euro Qualifier
20/11/74	England v. Portugal	0-0	Euro Qualifier
04/12/74	Oxford University v. Cambridge University	3-1	Varsity Match
01/03/75	Aston Villa v. Norwich City	1-0	League Cup Final
12/03/75	England v. West Germany	2-0	Friendly
22/03/75	England v. The Netherlands	4-0	Schoolboy International
16/04/75	England v. Cyprus	5-0	Euro Qualifier
19/04/75	Hoddesdon Town v. Epson & Ewell	2-1	F.A. Vase Final
26/04/75	Matlock Town v. Scarborough	4-0	F.A. Trophy Final
03/05/75	West Ham United v. Fulham	2-0	F.A. Cup Final
21/05/75	England v. Wales	2-2	Home International
24/05/75	England v. Scotland	5-1	Home International
07/06/75	England v. Scotland	0-1	Schoolboy International
08/06/75	Plymouth v. Merseyside	3-1	N.A. of Youth Clubs Cup
10/08/75	Derby County v. West Ham United	2-0	F.A. Charity Shield
03/12/75	Oxford University v. Cambridge University	2-0	Varsity Match
28/02/76	Manchester City v. Newcastle United	2-1	League Cup Final
20/03/76	England v. Wales	4-1	Schoolboy International
10/04/76	Billericay Town v. Stamford	1-0	F.A. Vase Final
24/04/76	Scarborough v. Stafford Rangers	3-2	F.A. Trophy Final
01/05/76	Southampton v. Manchester United	1-0	F.A. Cup Final
11/05/76	England v. Northern Ireland	4-0	Home International
05/06/76	England v. France	6-1	Schoolboy International
14/08/76	Liverpool v. Southampton	1-0	F.A. Charity Shield
08/09/76	England v. Republic Of Ireland	1-1	Friendly
13/10/76	England v. Finland	2-1	World Cup Qualifier
08/12/76	Cambridge University v. Oxford University	0-0	Varsity Match
09/02/77	England v. The Netherlands	0-2	Friendly

12/03/77	Aston Villa v. Everton	0-0 (aet)	League Cup Final
19/03/77	England v. Scotland	2-0	Schoolboy International
30/03/77	England v. Luxembourg	5-0	World Cup Qualifier
30/04/77	Billericay Town v. Sheffield	1-1 (aet)	F.A. Vase Final
14/05/77	Scarborough v. Dagenham	2-1	F.A. Trophy Final
21/05/77	Manchester United v. Liverpool	2-1	F.A. Cup Final
31/05/77	England v. Wales	0-1	Home International
04/06/77	England v. Scotland	1-2	Home International
18/06/77	England v. West Germany	1-2	Schoolboy International
13/08/77	Liverpool v. Manchester United	0-0	F.A. Charity Shield
07/09/77	England v. Switzerland	0-0	Friendly
16/11/77	England v. Italy	2-0	World Cup Qualifier
07/12/77	Oxford University v. Cambridge University	4-0	Varsity Match
04/03/78	England v. France	3-3	Schoolboy International
18/03/78	Nottingham Forest v. Liverpool	0-0 (aet)	League Cup Final
19/04/78	England v. Brazil	1-1	Friendly
22/04/78	Blue Star v. Barton Rovers	2-1	F.A. Vase Final
29/04/78	Altrincham v. Leatherhead	3-1	F.A. Trophy Final
06/05/78	Ipswich Town v. Arsenal	1-0	F.A. Cup Final
10/05/78	Liverpool v. Bruges (Belgium)	1-0	European Cup Final
16/05/78	England v. Northern Ireland	1-0	Home International
24/05/78	England v. Hungary	4-1	Friendly
27/05/78	England v. Scotland	3-1	Schoolboy International
12/08/78	Nottingham Forest v. Ipswich Town	5-0	F.A. Charity Shield
29/11/78	England v. Czechoslovakia	1-0	Friendly
06/12/78	Cambridge University v. Oxford University	2-1	Varsity Match
07/02/79	England v. Northern Ireland	4-0	Euro Qualifier
17/03/79	Nottingham Forest v. Southampton	3-2	League Cup Final
24/03/79	England v. Wales	1-1	Schoolboy International
28/04/79	Billericay Town v. Almondsbury Greenway	4-1	F.A. Vase Final
12/05/79	Arsenal v. Manchester United	3-2	F.A. Cup Final
19/05/79	Stafford Rangers v. Kettering Town	2-0	F.A. Trophy Final
23/05/79	England v. Wales	0-0	Home International
26/05/79	England v. Scotland	3-1	Home International
09/06/79	England v. West Germany	2-2	Schoolboy International
11/08/79	Liverpool v. Arsenal	3-1	F.A. Charity Shield
12/09/79	England v. Denmark	1-0	Euro Qualifier
22/11/79	England v. Bulgaria	2-0	Euro Qualifier
05/12/79	Oxford University v. Cambridge University	3-1	Varsity Match
06/02/80	England v. Republic Of Ireland	2-0	Euro Qualifier
15/03/80	Wolverhampton Wdrs v. Nottingham Forest	1-0	League Cup Final
22/03/80	England v. Switzerland	2-0	Schoolboy International
26/04/80	Stamford v. Guisborough Town	2-0	F.A. Vase Final
10/05/80	West Ham United v. Arsenal	1-0	F.A. Cup Final
13/05/80	England v. Argentina	3-1	Friendly
17/05/80	Dagenham v. Mossley	2-1	F.A. Trophy Final
20/05/80	England v. Northern Ireland	1-1	Home International
07/06/80	England v. Scotland	4-5	Schoolboy International
09/08/80	Liverpool v. West Ham United	1-0	F.A. Charity Shield
10/09/80	England v. Norway	4-0	World Cup Qualifier
30/10/80	Enfield Town v. Harrow Borough	2-1	Isthmian League
19/11/80	England v. Switzerland	2-1	World Cup Qualifier
10/12/80	Oxford University v. Cambridge University	2-0	Varsity Match
14/03/81	Liverpool v. West Ham United	1-1 (aet)	League Cup Final
25/03/81	England v. Spain	1-2	Friendly
28/03/81	England v. Northern Ireland	4-0	Schoolboy Int'l (Victory Cup)
25/04/81	Whickham v. Willenhall Town	3-2	F.A. Vase Final
29/04/81	England v. Romania	0-0	World Cup Qualifier
09/05/81	Tottenham Hotspur v. Manchester City	1-1 (aet)	F.A. Cup Final
12/05/81	England v. Brazil	0-1	Friendly
14/05/81	Tottenham Hotspur v. Manchester City	3-2	F.A. Cup Final Replay
16/05/81	Bishops Stortford v. Sutton United	1-0	F.A. Trophy Final
20/05/81	England v. Wales	0-0	Home International
23/05/81	England v. Scotland	0-1	Home International
13/06/81	England v. West Germany	1-2	Schoolboy International
22/08/81	Aston Villa v. Tottenham Hotspur	2-2	F.A. Charity Shield
18/11/81	England v. Hungary	1-0	World Cup Qualifier
09/12/81	Oxford University v. Cambridge University	2-0	Varsity Match
23/02/82	England v. Northern Ireland	4-0	Home International

13/03/82	Liverpool v. Tottenham Hotspur	3-1 (aet)	League Cup Final
05/05/82	England v. The Netherlands	7-0	Schoolboy International
08/05/82	Forest Grn Rov. v. Rainworth Miners Welfare	3-0	F.A. Vase Final
15/05/82	Enfield Town v. Altrincham	1-0	F.A. Trophy Final
22/05/82	Tottenham Hotspur v. Queens Park Rangers	1-1 (aet)	F.A. Cup Final
25/05/82	England v. The Netherlands	2-0	Friendly
27/05/82	Tottenham Hotspur v. Queens Park Rangers	1-0	F.A. Cup Final Replay
05/06/82	England v. Scotland	0-0	Schoolboy International
21/08/82	Liverpool v. Tottenham Hotspur	1-0	F.A. Charity Shield
13/10/82	England v. West Germany	1-2	Friendly
08/12/82	Oxford University v. Cambridge University	4-2	Varsity Match
15/12/82	England v. Luxembourg	9-0	Euro Qualifier
23/02/83	England v. Wales	2-1	Home International
19/03/83	England v. West Germany	1-0	Schoolboy International
26/03/83	Liverpool v. Manchester United	2-1 (aet)	Milk (League) Cup Final
30/03/83	England v. Greece	0-0	Euro Qualifier
27/04/83	England v. Hungary	2-0	Euro Qualifier
30/04/83	Valley Sports Rugby v. Halesowen Town	1-0	F.A. Vase Final
14/05/83	Telford United v. Northwich Victoria	2-1	F.A. Trophy Final
21/05/83	Manchester United v. Brighton & Hove Albion	2-2 (aet)	F.A. Cup Final
26/05/83	Manchester United v. Brighton & Hove Albion	4-0	F.A. Cup Final Replay
01/06/83	England v. Scotland	2-0	Home International
11/06/83	England v. Scotland	3-3	Schoolboy International
20/08/83	Manchester United v. Liverpool	2-0	F.A. Charity Shield
21/09/83	England v. Denmark	0-1	Euro Qualifier
07/12/83	Oxford University v. Cambridge University	2-2	Varsity Match
17/03/84	England v. Scotland	1-0	Schoolboy International
25/03/84	Liverpool v. Everton	0-0 (aet)	Milk (League) Cup Final
04/04/84	England v. Northern Ireland	1-0	Home International
28/04/84	Stansted v. Stamford	3-2	F.A. Vase Final
12/05/84	Bangor City v. Northwich Victoria	1-1 (aet)	F.A. Trophy Final
19/05/84	Everton v. Watford	2-0	F.A. Cup Final
02/06/84	England v. USSR	0-2	Friendly
09/06/84	England v. The Netherlands	4-1	Schoolboy International
18/08/84	Everton v. Liverpool	1-0	F.A. Charity Shield
12/09/84	England v. East Germany	1-0	Friendly
17/10/84	England v. Finland	5-0	World Cup Qualifier
12/12/84	Cambridge University v. Oxford University	4-2	Varsity Match
16/03/85	England v. West Germany	0-1	Schoolboy International
24/03/85	Norwich City v. Sunderland	1-0	Milk (League) Cup Final
26/03/85	England v. Republic Of Ireland	2-1	Friendly
27/04/85	Halesowen Town v. Fleetwood Town	3-1	F.A. Vase Final
11/05/85	Wealdstone v. Boston United	2-1	F.A. Trophy Final
18/05/85	Manchester United v. Everton	1-0 (aet)	F.A. Cup Final
01/06/85	Wigan Athletic v. Brentford	3-1	Freight Rover Trophy Final
08/06/85	England v. Switzerland	2-0	Schoolboy International
09/06/85	England v. Yugoslavia	3-2	U16 International
10/08/85	Everton v. Manchester United	2-0	F.A. Charity Shield
11/09/85	England v. Romania	1-1	World Cup Qualifier
16/10/85	England v. Turkey	5-0	World Cup Qualifier
13/11/85	England v. Northern Ireland	0-0	World Cup Qualifier
11/12/85	Cambridge University v. Oxford University	2-0	Varsity Match
08/03/86	England v. The Netherlands	1-0	Schoolboy International
23/03/86	Chelsea v. Manchester City	5-4	Full Members Cup Final
20/04/86	Oxford United v. Queens Park Rangers	3-0	Milk (League) Cup Final
23/04/86	England v. Scotland	2-1	Rous Cup (Friendly)
26/04/86	Halesowen Town v. Southall	3-0	F.A. Vase Final
10/05/86	Liverpool v. Everton	3-1	F.A. Cup Final
17/05/86	Altrincham v. Runcorn	1-0	F.A. Trophy Final
24/05/86	Bristol City v. Bolton Wanderers	3-0	Freight Rover Trophy Final
29/05/86	England v. France	0-1	U16 International
31/05/86	England v. Italy	2-1	Schoolboy International
16/08/86	Everton v. Liverpool	1-1	F.A. Charity Shield
15/10/86	England v. Northern Ireland	3-0	Euro Qualifier
12/11/86	England v. Yugoslavia	2-0	Euro Qualifier
04/12/86	Cambridge University v. Oxford University	4-3	Varsity Match
14/03/87	England v. West Germany	2-0	Schoolboy International
29/03/87	Blackburn Rovers v. Charlton Athletic	1-0	Full Members Cup Final
05/04/87	Arsenal v. Liverpool	2-1 (aet)	Littlewoods (League) Cup

Date	Match	Score	Competition
25/04/87	St Helens Town v. Warrington Town	3-2	F.A. Vase Final
09/05/87	Burton Albion v. Kidderminster Harriers	0-0 (aet)	F.A. Trophy Final
16/05/87	Coventry City v. Tottenham Hotspur	3-2 (aet)	F.A. Cup Final
19/05/87	England v. Brazil	1-1	Rous Cup (Friendly)
24/05/87	Mansfield Town v. Bristol City	1-1 (5-4pen)	Freight Rover Trophy Final)
30/05/87	England v. Scotland	1-1	Schoolboy Int'l (Victory Cup)
01/08/87	England v. The Netherlands	3-1	U17 International
01/08/87	Everton v. Coventry City	1-0	F.A. Charity Shield
08/08/87	England v. Denmark	2-1	U16 International
08/08/87	Football League XI v. Rest of World	3-0	Football League Centenary
14/10/87	England v. Turkey	8-0	Euro Qualifier
09/12/87	Cambridge University v. Oxford University	2-1	Varsity Match
12/03/88	England v. Brazil	2-0	Schoolboy International
23/03/88	England v. The Netherlands	2-2	Friendly
27/03/88	Reading v. Luton Town	4-1	Simod Cup Final
16/04/88	League Centenary T/ment (16 clubs - k.o.)		Football League Centenary
17/04/88	League Centenary T/ment, won by Notts Forest		Football League Centenary
23/04/88	Colne Dynamoes v. Emley	1-0 (aet)	F.A. Vase Final
24/04/88	Luton Town v. Arsenal	3-2	Littlewoods (League) Cup
07/05/88	Enfield Town v. Telford United	0-0 (aet)	F.A. Trophy Final
14/05/88	Wimbledon v. Liverpool	1-0	F.A. Cup Final
21/05/88	England v. Scotland	1-0	Rous Cup (Friendly)
24/05/88	England v. Colombia	1-1	Rous Cup (Friendly)
28/05/88	England v. Italy	4-1	Schoolboy International
29/05/88	Wolverhampton Wanderers v Burnley	2-0	Sherpa Vans Trophy Final
06/06/88	Hendon v. Wembley	2-0	Middlesex Charity Cup Final
13/08/88	Milan (Italy) v. Tottenham Hotspur	2-1	Wembley International Tournament
13/08/88	Arsenal v. Tottenham Hotspur	4-0	as above (WIT)
14/08/88	Arsenal v. Bayern Munich (W. Germany)	3-0	as above (WIT)
14/08/88	Milan (Italy) v. Bayern Munich (W. Germany)	1-0	as above (WIT)
17/08/88	England v. Israel	1-1	U16 International
20/08/88	Liverpool v. Wimbledon	2-1	F.A. Charity Shield
14/09/88	England v. Denmark	1-0	Friendly
19/10/88	England v. Sweden	0-0	World Cup Qualifier
11/03/89	England v. Belgium	3-1	Schoolboy International
09/04/89	Nottingham Forest v. Luton Town	3-1	Littlewoods (League) Cup
26/04/89	England v. Albania	5-0	World Cup Qualifier
30/04/89	Nottingham Forest v. Everton	4-3 (aet)	Simod Cup Final
06/05/89	Sudbury Town v. Tamworth	1-1 (aet)	F.A. Vase Final
13/05/89	Telford United v. Macclesfield Town	1-0	F.A. Trophy Final
20/05/89	Liverpool v. Everton	3-2 (aet)	F.A. Cup Final
23/05/89	England v. Chile	0-0	Rous Cup (Friendly)
23/05/89	England v. Sweden	0-2	Womens International
28/05/89	Bolton Wanderers v. Torquay United	4-1	Sherpa Vans Trophy Final
03/06/89	England v. Poland	3-0	World Cup Qualifier
10/06/89	England v. West Germany	1-3	Schoolboy International
29/07/89	Arsenal v. Porto (Portugal)	1-0	Makita Tournament
29/07/89	Liverpool v. Dynamo Kiev (USSR)	2-0	Makita Tournament
30/07/89	Dynamo Kiev (USSR) v. Porto (Portugal)	1-0	Makita Tournament
30/07/89	Arsenal v. Liverpool	1-0	Makita Tournament
11/08/89	England v. Scandinavia	2-1	U16 International
12/08/89	Liverpool v. Arsenal	1-0	F.A. Charity Shield
15/11/89	England v. Italy	0-0	Friendly
13/12/89	England v. Yugoslavia	2-1	Friendly
18/03/90	England v. France	1-1	Schoolboy International
25/03/90	Chelsea v. Middlesbrough	1-0	Zenith Data Systems Cup
28/03/90	England v. Brazil	1-0	Friendly
28/03/90	England v. Denmark	0-0	U18 International
25/04/90	England v. Czechoslovakia	4-2	Friendly
25/04/90	England v. Czechoslovakia	1-1	U18 International
29/04/90	Nottingham Forest v. Oldham Athletic	1-0	Littlewoods (League) Cup
05/05/90	Bridlington Town v. Yeading	0-0 (aet)	F.A. Vase Final
12/05/90	Manchester United v. Crystal Palace	3-3 (aet)	F.A. Cup Final
15/05/90	England v. Poland	3-0	U18 International
15/05/90	England v. Denmark	1-0	Friendly
17/05/90	Manchester United v. Crystal Palace	1-0	F.A. Cup Final Replay
19/05/90	Barrow v. Leek Town	3-0	F.A. Trophy Final
20/05/90	Tranmere Rovers v. Bristol Rovers	2-1	Leyland DAF Trophy Final
22/05/90	England v. France	1-3	U17 International

22/05/90	England v. Uruguay	1-2	Friendly
26/05/90	Cambridge United v. Chesterfield	1-0	Promotion Play-Off Final
27/05/90	Notts County v. Tranmere Rovers	2-0	Promotion Play-Off Final
28/05/90	Swindon Town v. Sunderland	1-0	Promotion Play-Off Final
02/06/90	England v. The Netherlands	1-0	Schoolboy International
10/08/90	Sampdoria (Italy) v. Real Sociedad (Spain)	1-1 (5-3pen)	Makita Tournament
10/08/90	Arsenal v. Aston Villa	2-0	Makita Tournament
11/08/90	Real Sociedad (Spain) v. Aston Villa	1-0	Makita Tournament
11/08/90	Sampdoria (Italy) v. Arsenal	1-0	Makita Tournament
18/08/90	Liverpool v. Manchester United	1-1	F.A. Charity Shield
12/09/90	England v. Hungary	1-0	Friendly
17/10/90	England v. Poland	2-0	Euro Qualifier
06/02/91	England v. Cameroon	2-0	Friendly
09/03/91	England v. Scotland	2-1	Schoolboy International
27/03/91	England v. Republic Of Ireland	1-1	Euro Qualifier
07/04/91	Crystal Palace v. Everton	4-1	Zenith Data Systems Cup
14/04/91	Tottenham Hotspur v. Arsenal	3-1	F.A. Cup Semi Final
21/04/91	Sheffield Wednesday v. Manchester United	1-0	Rumbelows (League) Cup Final
04/05/91	Guiseley v. Gresley Rovers	4-4 (aet)	F.A. Vase Final
11/05/91	Wycombe Wanderers v. Kidderminster Harriers	2-1	F.A. Trophy Final
18/05/91	Tottenham Hotspur v. Nottingham Forest	2-1 (aet)	F.A. Cup Final
21/05/91	England v. USSR	3-1	Friendly
25/05/91	England v. Argentina	2-2	Friendly
25/05/91	England v. Spain	1-1	U19 International
26/05/91	Birmingham City v. Tranmere Rovers	3-2	Leyland DAF Trophy Final
31/05/91	Torquay United v. Blackpool	2-2 (5-4pen)	Promotion Play-Off Final
01/06/91	Tranmere Rovers v. Bolton Wanderers	1-0 (aet)	Promotion Play-Off Final
02/06/91	Notts County v. Brighton & Hove Albion	3-1	Promotion Play-Off Final
08/06/91	England v. West Germany	1-3	Schoolboy International
10/08/91	Arsenal v. Tottenham Hotspur	0-0	F.A. Charity Shield
11/09/91	England v. Germany	0-1	Friendly
16/10/91	England v. Turkey	1-0	Euro Qualifier
19/02/92	England v. France	2-0	Friendly
07/03/92	England v. The Netherlands	0-0	Schoolboy International
29/03/92	Nottingham Forest v. Southampton	3-2 (aet)	Zenith Data Systems Cup
12/04/92	Manchester United v. Nottingham Forest	1-0	Rumbelows (League) Cup Final
25/04/92	Wimborne Town v. Guiseley	5-3	F.A. Vase Final
09/05/92	Liverpool v. Sunderland	2-0	F.A. Cup Final
10/05/92	Colchester United v. Witton Albion	3-1	F.A. Trophy Final
16/05/92	Stoke City v. Stockport County	1-0	Autoglass Trophy Final
17/05/92	England v. Brazil	1-1	Friendly
20/05/92	Barcelona (Spain) v. Sampdoria (Italy)	1-0 (aet)	European Cup Final
23/05/92	Blackpool v. Scunthorpe United	1-1 (4-3pen)	Promotion Play-Off Final
24/05/92	Peterborough Utd v. Stockport County	2-1	Promotion Play-Off Final
25/05/92	Blackburn Rovers v. Leicester City	1-0	Promotion Play-Off Final
06/06/92	England v. Italy	1-1	Schoolboy International
08/08/92	Leeds United v. Liverpool	4-3	F.A. Charity Shield
14/10/92	England v. Norway	1-1	World Cup Qualifier
18/11/92	England v. Turkey	4-0	World Cup Qualifier
17/02/93	England v. San Marino	6-0	World Cup Qualifier
13/03/93	England v. Scotland	1-2	Schoolboy Int'l (Victory Cup)
27/03/93	Cremonese (Italy) v. Derby County	3-1 (aet)	Anglo-Italian Cup
03/04/93	Sheffield Wednesday v. Sheffield United	2-1	F.A. Cup Semi-Final
04/04/93	Arsenal v. Tottenham Hotspur	1-0	F.A. Cup Semi-Final
18/04/93	Arsenal v. Sheffield Wednesday	2-1	Coca-Cola (League) Cup Final
28/04/93	England v. The Netherlands	2-2	World Cup Qualifier
08/05/93	Bridlington Town v. Tiverton Town	1-0	F.A. Vase Final
09/05/93	Wycombe Wanderers v. Runcorn	4-1	F.A. Trophy Final
12/05/93	Parma (Italy) v. Royal Antwerp (Belgium)	3-1	European Cup Winners Cup
15/05/93	Arsenal v. Sheffield Wednesday	1-1 (aet)	F.A. Cup Final
20/05/93	Arsenal v. Sheffield Wednesday	2-1	F.A. Cup Final Replay
22/05/93	Port Vale v. Stockport County	2-1	Autoglass Trophy Final
23/05/93	Arsenal v. Knowsley United	3-0	Womens League Cup Final
29/05/93	York City v. Crewe Alexandra	1-1 (5-3pen)	Promotion Play-Off Final
30/05/93	West Bromwich Albion v. Port Vale	3-0	Promotion Play-Off Final
31/05/93	Swindon Town v. Leicester City	4-3	Promotion Play-Off Final
12/06/93	England v. Germany	0-0	Schoolboy International
07/08/93	Manchester United v. Arsenal	1-1 (5-4pen)	F.A. Charity Shield
08/09/93	England v. Poland	3-0	World Cup Qualifier

09/03/94	England v. Denmark	1-0	Friendly
12/03/94	England v. Switzerland	3-0	Schoolboy International
20/03/94	Brescia (Italy) v. Notts County	1-0	Anglo-Italian Cup
27/03/94	Aston Villa v. Manchester United	3-1	Coca-Cola (League) Cup Final
09/04/94	Chelsea v. Luton Town	2-0	F.A. Cup Semi-Final
10/04/94	Manchester United v. Oldham Athletic	1-1 (aet)	F.A. Cup Semi-Final
24/04/94	Swansea City v. Huddersfield Town	1-1 (3-1pen)	Autoglass Trophy Final
07/05/94	Diss Town v. Taunton Town	2-1 (aet)	F.A. Vase Final
14/05/94	Manchester United v. Chelsea	4-0	F.A. Cup Final
17/05/94	England v. Greece	5-0	Friendly
21/05/94	Woking v. Runcorn	2-1	F.A. Trophy Final
22/05/94	England v. Norway	0-0	Friendly
28/05/94	Wycombe Wanderers v. Preston North End	4-2	Promotion Play-Off Final
29/05/94	Burnley v. Stockport County	2-1	Promotion Play-Off Final
30/05/94	Leicester City v. Derby County	2-1	Promotion Play-Off Final
16/06/94	England v. France	2-1	Schoolboy International
14/08/94	Manchester United v. Blackburn Rovers	2-0	F.A. Charity Shield
07/09/94	England v. USA	2-0	Friendly
12/10/94	England v. Romania	1-1	Friendly
16/11/94	England v. Nigeria	1-0	Friendly
15/03/95	England v. Brazil	1-0	Schoolboy International
19/03/95	Notts County v. Ascoli (Italy)	2-1	Anglo-Italian Cup
29/03/95	England v. Uruguay	0-0	Friendly
02/04/95	Liverpool v. Bolton Wanderers	2-1	Coca-Cola (League) Cup Final
23/04/95	Birmingham City v. Carlisle United	1-0	Auto Windscreens Shield
13/05/95	Arlesey Town v. Oxford City	2-1	F.A. Vase Final
14/05/95	Woking v. Kidderminster Harriers	2-1	F.A. Trophy Final
20/05/95	Everton v. Manchester United	1-0	F.A. Cup Final
27/05/95	Chesterfield v. Bury	2-0	Promotion Play-Off Final
28/05/95	Huddersfield Town v. Bristol Rovers	2-1	Promotion Play-Off Final
29/05/95	Bolton Wanderers v. Reading	4-3 (aet)	Promotion Play-Off Final
03/06/95	England v. Japan	2-1	Friendly
10/06/95	England v. Germany	2-4	Schoolboy International
11/06/95	England v. Brazil	1-3	Friendly
13/08/95	Everton v. Blackburn Rovers	1-0	F.A. Charity Shield
06/09/95	England v. Colombia	0-0	Friendly
15/11/95	England v. Switzerland	3-1	Friendly
12/12/95	England v. Portugal	1-1	Friendly
09/03/96	England v. Spain	2-3	Schoolboy International
17/03/96	Genoa (Italy) v. Port Vale	5-2	Anglo-Italian Cup
24/03/96	Aston Villa v. Leeds United	3-0	Coca-Cola (League) Cup Final
27/03/96	England v. Bulgaria	1-0	Friendly
14/04/96	Rotherham United v. Shrewsbury Town	2-1	Auto Windscreens Shield
24/04/96	England v. Croatia	0-0	Friendly
11/05/96	Manchester United v. Liverpool	1-0	F.A. Cup Final
12/05/96	Brigg Town v. Clitheroe	3-0	F.A. Vase Final
18/05/96	England v. Hungary	3-0	Friendly
19/05/96	Macclesfield Town v. Northwich Victoria	3-1	F.A. Trophy Final
25/05/96	Plymouth Argyle v. Darlington	1-0	Promotion Play-Off Final
26/05/96	Bradford City v. Notts County	2-0	Promotion Play-Off Final
27/05/96	Leicester City v. Crystal Palace	2-1 (aet)	Promotion Play-Off Final
08/06/96	England v. Switzerland	1-1	Euro '96 Group Match
15/06/96	England v. Scotland	2-0	Euro '96 Group Match
18/06/96	England v. The Netherlands	4-1	Euro '96 Group Match
22/06/96	England v. Spain	0-0 (4-2pen)	Euro '96 Qtr-Final
26/06/96	England v. Germany	1-1 (5-6pen)	Euro '96 Semi-Final
30/06/96	Germany v. Czech Republic	2-1 (aet)	Euro '96 Final
11/08/96	Manchester United v. Newcastle United	4-0	F.A. Charity Shield
12/08/96	Brigade Bodega v. Dawlish Town	1-0	Carlsberg Pub Cup International
09/10/96	England v. Poland	2-1	World Cup Qualifier
12/02/97	England v. Italy	1-0	World Cup Qualifier
29/03/97	England v. Mexico	2-0	Friendly
06/04/97	Leicester City v. Middlesbrough	1-1 (aet)	Coca-Cola (League) Cup Final
20/04/97	Carlisle United v. Colchester United	0-0 (4-3pen)	Auto Windscreens Shield
30/04/97	England v. Georgia	2-0	World Cup Qualifier
10/05/97	Poulton Victoria v. Corby Caledonian	3-1	Carlsberg Pub Cup Final
10/05/97	Whitby Town v. North Ferriby United	3-0	F.A. Vase Final
17/05/97	Chelsea v. Middlesbrough	2-0	F.A. Cup Final
18/05/97	Woking v. Dagenham & Redbridge	1-0 (aet)	F.A. Trophy Final

Date	Match	Score	Competition
24/05/97	Northampton Town v. Swansea City	1-0	Promotion Play-Off Final
25/05/97	Crewe Alexandra v. Brentford	1-0	Promotion Play-Off Final
26/05/97	Crystal Palace v. Sheffield United	1-0	Promotion Play-Off Final
07/06/97	England v. Germany	2-1	Schoolboy International
03/08/97	Manchester United v. Chelsea	1-1 (4-2pen)	F.A. Charity Shield
10/09/97	England v. Moldova	4-0	World Cup Qualifier
15/11/97	England v. Cameroon	2-0	Friendly
11/02/98	England v. Chile	0-2	Friendly
14/03/98	England v. Brazil	0-0	Schoolboy International
29/03/98	Chelsea v. Middlesbrough	2-0	Coca-Cola (League) Cup Final
19/04/98	Grimsby Town v. Bournemouth	2-1 (aet)	Auto Windscreens Shield
22/04/98	England v. Portugal	3-0	Friendly
09/05/98	West Hendon ESC v. Honiton Clyst	1-1 (3-1pen)	Carlsberg Pub Cup Final
09/05/98	Tiverton Town v. Tow Law Town	1-0	F.A. Vase Final
16/05/98	Arsenal v. Newcastle United	2-0	F.A. Cup Final
17/05/98	Cheltenham Town v. Southport	1-0	F.A. Trophy Final
22/05/98	Colchester United v. Torquay United	1-0	Promotion Play-Off Final
23/05/98	England v. Saudi Arabia	0-0	Friendly
24/05/98	Grimsby Town v. Northampton Town	1-0	Promotion Play-Off Final
25/05/98	Charlton Athletic v. Sunderland	4-4 (7-6pen)	Promotion Play-Off Final
20/06/98	West Hendon ESC v. Vagns Krostue (Denmark)	1-0	Carlsberg Pub Cup International
09/08/98	Arsenal v. Manchester United	3-0	F.A. Charity Shield
30/09/98	Arsenal v. Panathinaikos (Greece)	2-1	Champions League (Group)
10/10/98	England v. Bulgaria	0-0	Euro Qualifier
21/10/98	Arsenal v. Dynamo Kiev (Ukraine)	1-1	Champions League (Group)
18/11/98	England v. Czech Republic	2-0	Friendly
21/11/98	Arsenal v. Lens (France)	0-1	Champions League (Group)
10/02/99	England v. France	0-2	Friendly
21/03/99	Tottenham Hotspur v. Leicester City	1-0	Worthington (League) Cup
27/03/99	England v. Poland	3-1	Euro Qualifier
18/04/99	Wigan Athletic v. Millwall	1-0	Auto Windscreens Shield
08/05/99	England v. The Netherlands	1-2	Schoolboy International
15/05/99	Kingstonian v. Forest Green Rovers	1-0	F.A. Trophy Final
16/05/99	Sizewell v. West Hendon ESC	2-0	Carlsberg Pub Cup Final
16/05/99	Tiverton Town v. Bedlington Terriers	1-0	F.A. Vase Final
22/05/99	Manchester United v. Newcastle United	2-0	F.A. Cup Final
29/05/99	Scunthorpe United v. Leyton Orient	1-0	Promotion Play-Off Final
30/05/99	Manchester City v. Gillingham	2-2 (3-1pen)	Promotion Play-Off Final
31/05/99	Watford v. Bolton Wanderers	2-0	Promotion Play-Off Final
05/06/99	England v. Sweden	0-0	Euro Qualifier
04/07/99	England v. Scotland	5-0	U16 Girls International
04/07/99	England v. Argentina	2-1	U16 International
01/08/99	Arsenal v. Manchester United	2-1	F.A. Charity Shield
04/09/99	England v. Luxembourg	6-0	Euro Qualifier
22/09/99	Arsenal v. AIK Solna (Sweden)	3-1	Champions League (Group)
19/10/99	Arsenal v. Barcelona (Spain)	2-4	Champions League (Group)
27/10/99	Arsenal v. Fiorentina (Italy)	0-1	Champions League (Group)
17/11/99	England v. Scotland	0-1	Euro Qualifier
23/02/00	England v. Argentina	0-0	Friendly
27/02/00	Leicester City v. Tranmere Rovers	2-1	Worthington (League) Cup
01/04/00	England v. Hungary	0-1	U18 International
08/04/00	Aston Villa v. Bolton Wanderers	0-0 (4-1pen)	F.A. Cup Semi-Final
09/04/00	Chelsea v. Newcastle United	2-1	F.A. Cup Semi-Final
16/04/00	West Brom. Albion v. Scunthorpe Utd	0-0 (3-2pen)	League Youth Alliance Cup
16/04/00	Stoke City v. Bristol City	2-1	Auto Windscreens Shield
06/05/00	Earl Soham v. Eastleigh	2-1	Carlsberg Pub Cup Final
06/05/00	Deal Town v. Chippenham Town	1-0	F.A. Vase Final
13/05/00	Kingstonian v. Kettering Town	3-2	F.A. Trophy Final
20/05/00	Chelsea v. Aston Villa	1-0	F.A. Cup Final
26/05/00	Peterborough United v. Darlington	1-0	Promotion Play-Off Final
27/05/00	England v. Brazil	1-1	Friendly
28/05/00	Gillingham v. Wigan Athletic	3-2 (aet)	Promotion Play-Off Final
29/05/00	Ipswich Town v. Barnsley	4-2	Promotion Play-Off Final
31/05/00	England v. Ukraine	2-0	Friendly
13/08/00	Chelsea v. Manchester United	2-0	F.A. Charity Shield
07/10/00	England v. Germany	0-1	World Cup Qualifier

Rugby League Challenge Cup Finals at Wembley 1929 – 1999

04/05/29	Wigan 13	Dewsbury 2	
03/05/30	Widnes 10	St Helens 3	
02/05/31	Halifax 22	York 8	
06/05/33	Huddersfield 21	Warrington 17	
05/05/34	Hunslet 11	Widnes 5	
04/05/35	Castleford 11	Huddersfield 8	
02/05/36	Leeds 18	Warrington 2	
01/05/37	Widnes 18	Keighley 5	
07/05/38	Salford 7	Barrow 4	
06/05/39	Halifax 20	Salford 3	
04/05/46	Wakefield Trinity 13	Wigan 12	
03/05/47	Bradford Northern 8	Leeds 4	
01/05/48	Wigan 8	Bradford Northern 3	
07/05/49	Bradford Northern 12	Halifax 0	
06/05/50	Warrington 19	Widnes 0	
05/05/51	Wigan 10	Barrow 0	
19/04/52	Workington Town 18	Featherstone Rovers 10	
25/04/53	Huddersfield 15	St Helens 10	
24/04/54	Warrington 4	Halifax 4	

(Warrington won replay 8-4 at Odsal, Bradford)

30/04/55	Barrow 21	Workington Town 12	
28/04/56	St Helens 13	Halifax 2	
11/05/57	Leeds 9	Barrow 7	
10/05/58	Wigan 13	Workington Town 9	
09/05/59	Wigan 30	Hull 13	
14/05/60	Wakefield Trinity 38	Hull 5	
13/05/61	St Helens 12	Wigan 6	
12/05/62	Wakefield Trinity 12	Huddersfield 6	
11/05/63	Wakefield Trinity 25	Wigan 10	
09/05/64	Widnes 13	Hull Kingston Rovers 5	
08/05/65	Wigan 20	Hunslet 16	
21/05/66	St Helens 21	Wigan 2	
13/05/67	Featherstone Rovers 17	Barrow 12	
11/05/68	Leeds 11	Wakefield Trinity 10	
17/05/69	Castleford 11	Salford 6	
09/05/70	Castleford 7	Wigan 2	
15/05/71	Leigh 24	Leeds 7	
13/05/72	St.Helens 16	Leeds 13	
12/05/73	Featherstone Rovers 33	Bradford Northern 14	
11/05/74	Warrington 24	Featherstone Rovers 9	
10/05/75	Widnes 14	Warrington 7	
08/05/76	St.Helens 20	Widnes 5	
07/05/77	Leeds 16	Widnes 7	
13/05/78	Leeds 14	St Helens 12	
05/05/79	Widnes 12	Wakefield Trinity 3	
03/05/80	Hull Kingston Rovers 10	Hull 5	
02/05/81	Widnes 18	Hull Kingston Rovers 9	
01/05/82	Hull 14	Widnes 14	

(Hull won replay 18-9 at Elland Rd, Leeds)

07/05/83	Featherstone Rovers 14	Hull 12	
05/05/84	Widnes 19	Wigan 6	
04/05/85	Wigan 28	Hull 24	
03/05/86	Castleford 15	Hull Kingston Rovers 14	
02/05/87	Halifax 19	St.Helens 18	
02/05/88	Wigan 32	Halifax 12	
29/04/89	Wigan 27	St Helens 0	
28/04/90	Wigan 36	Warrington 14	
27/04/91	Wigan 13	St.Helens 8	
02/05/92	Wigan 28	Castleford 12	
01/05/93	Wigan 20	Widnes 14	
30/04/94	Wigan 26	Leeds 16	
25/04/95	Wigan 30	Leeds 10	
27/04/96	St Helens 40	Bradford Bulls 32	
03/05/97	St Helens 32	Bradford Bulls 22	
02/05/98	Sheffield Eagles 17	Wigan Warriors 8	
01/05/99	Leeds Rhinos 52	London Broncos 16	

Notes: The 1932 final was held at Wigan. There was no competition in 1940. The 1941 to 1945 finals were held at club grounds in the north of England.

Most Wembley Final wins:

Wigan	15
St Helens	7
Widnes	7
Leeds/Leeds Rhinos	6
Castleford	4
Wakefield Trinity	4

Most Wembley Final Appearances:

Wigan	22
St Helens	13
Widnes	13
Leeds/Leeds Rhinos	11
Halifax	7
Warrington	7

Highest points total in a final:
72 points for St Helens v. Bradford Bulls in 1996

Highest points total for a team:
52 points for Leeds Rhinos against London Broncos in 1999

Biggest Winning Margin:
36 points for Leeds Rhinos against London Broncos in 1999

Highest points score by a losing team:
32 points for Bradford Bulls against St Helens in 1996

1972	The London Rock & Roll Show: Little Richard, Chuck Berry, Bill Haley & The Comets, Jerry Lee Lewis, Bo Diddley, Wizzard
1974	Crosby, Stills, Nash & Young, plus Joni Mitchell, The Band
1975	Elton John
1977	Elton John
	The Eagles
1979	The Who
1982	Rolling Stones
	Simon & Garfunkel
1984	Bob Dylan
	Elton John (Day & Night Concert)
1985	Bruce Springsteen
	LIVE AID - Status Quo, Queen, Dire Straits, Phil Collins, Elton John, U2, Bryan Ferry, David Bowie, Spandau Ballet, Wham!
1986	Wham!
	Queen plus Status Quo
1987	U2
	Phil Collins
	David Bowie (Glass Spider tour), plus Big Country
	Genesis (Invisible Touch tour)
	Madonna
1988	Nelsons Mandela's 70th Birthday Concert: Simple Minds, Peter Gabriel, Mahlathini, Mahotella Queens
	Michael Jackson ('Bad' World tour)
	Pink Floyd 'Delicate Sound of Thunder'
	Bruce Springsteen
	Amnesty International Benefit
1989	Bros
	Simple Minds
	Cliff Richard
1990	Rolling Stones
	Nelson Mandela Tribute
	Fleetwood Mac plus Jethro Tull, Hall & Oates
	Amitabh Bachchan
	Madonna
1991	Rod Stewart plus Joe Cocker, Status Quo
	INXS (Live Baby Live)
	Guns 'n' Roses
1992	Elton John plus Eric Clapton
	Michael Jackson
	Freddie Mercury Tribute
	Simply Red
	Bryan Adams
	Guns 'n' Roses
1993	Madonna
	Jean Michel Jarre
	Prince
	U2 (Zooropa Tour)
1995	Rod Stewart
	Rolling Stones
	Bon Jovi ('These Days' tour)
1996	Tina Turner
	The Eagles ('Hell Freezes Over' tour)
	The Three Tenors
1997	Songs and Visions
	Champion Of The World Christian Festival: Noel Richards plus Delerious, Sue Richards
	U2 (Pop Mart tour)
	Michael Jackson ('HIStory' tour)
1998	Spice Girls
	Elton John
	Bee Gees
1999	Aerosmith ('Toxic Twin Towers tour')
	Rolling Stones
	Celine Dion
	NetAid: David Bowie, Robbie Williams, Stereophonics, George Michael, Bryan Adams
2000	Oasis
	Tina Turner
	Bon Jovi (Crush tour), plus Toploader

World Speedway Championship Winners at Wembley

INDIVIDUAL CHAMPIONSHIPS 1936-1981

Year	Winner	Nationality
1936	Lionel Van Praag	Australia
1937	Jack Milne	USA
1938	Bluey Wilkinson	Australia
1949	Tommy Price	Great Britain
1950	Freddie Williams	Great Britain
1951	Jack Young	Australia
1952	Jack Young	Australia
1953	Freddie Williams	Great Britain
1954	Ronnie Moore	New Zealand
1955	Peter Craven	Great Britain
1956	Ove Fundin	Sweden
1957	Barry Briggs	New Zealand
1958	Barry Briggs	New Zealand
1959	Ronnie Moore	New Zealand
1960	Ove Fundin	Sweden
1962	Peter Craven	Great Britain
1963	Ove Fundin	Sweden
1965	Björn Knutsson	Sweden
1967	Ove Fundin	Sweden
1969	Ivan Mauger	New Zealand
1972	Ivan Mauger	New Zealand
1975	Ole Olsen	Denmark
1978	Ole Olsen	Denmark
1981	Bruce Penhall	USA

Competition was suspended during World War Two.

Most wins at Wembley:

Ove Fundin (Swed)	4
Barry Briggs (NZ)	2
Peter Craven (GB)	2
van Mauger (NZ)	2
Ronnie Moore (NZ)	2
Ole Olson (Den)	2
Freddie Williams (GB)	2
Jack Young (Aus)	2

TEAM CHAMPIONSHIPS 1968-1981

Year	Winners	Team Members
1968	Great Britain	Briggs, Mauger, Boocock, Ashby, Hunter
1970	Sweden	Fundin, Michanek, Jansson, Sjoesten
1973	Great Britain	Wilson, Betts, Collins, Simmons

Books
Adams, Tony & Riddley, Ian, *Addicted*, Harper Collins, 1999
Baddiel, Ivor, *Ultimate Football*, Dorling Kindersley, 1998
Cullis, Stan, *All For The Wolves*, Rupert Hart Davies, London, 1960
Banks, Gordon, *Banksy*, Michael Joseph Penguin, 2002
Bass, Howard, *Glorious Wembley*, Guiness Superlatives Ltd, 1985
Betjeman, John, 'Harrow on the Hill' from *Collected Poems*, John Murray Ltd, 1958
British Empire Exhibition 1924 – Official Guide
Charles, John. with Harris, Bob, *King John*, Headline, 2003
Chronicle of the Olympics 1896-1996, Dorling Kindersley, 1996
Edworthy, Niall, *England: The Official F.A. History*, Virgin Books, 1997
Gate, Robert, *An Illustrated History of Rugby League*, Weidenfeld, 1989
Gearing, Brian, & McNeill, Phil, (eds), *Seventy Years of BBC Sport*, Andre Deutsch, 1998
Green, Alan., *The Green Line*, Headline, 2000
Greenberg, Stan, *Whitaker's Olympic Almanack 2004*, A & C Black Ltd, 2003
Hewlett, Geoffrey (ed.), *A History Of Wembley*, Brent Library Service, 1979
Hoddle, Glenn, & Radnedge, Keir, *Five A Side Football*, Pelham Books, 1984
The Jimmy Seed Story, Phoenix Sports Books, 1957
Lloyd, Guy & Holt, Nick, *The F.A. Cup - The Complete Story*, Aurum, 2005
Merulli, Annabel, & Wenbourn, Neil, (eds), *British Sporting Greats*, Cassell Illustrated, 2002
Metroland (1924 edition) Facsimilie Edition, Southbank Publishing, 2004
Mitchell, Graham, The Roaring Twenties, B.T. Batsford, 1996
Moorhouse, Geoffrey, *A People's Game, The Official History of Rugby League 1895-1995*, Hodder and Stoughton, 1995
Morris, Graham, *Hero, Rugby League's Greatest Awards Winners*, Vertical Editions, 2005
Mourant, Andrew, & Rollin, Jack, *The Essential History of England*, Headline, 2004
The Olympics, Weidenfeld and Nicolson, 2004
Revie, Alistair, *All Roads Lead To Wembley*, Pelham Books Ltd, 1971
Robson, Bobby, & Hayward, Paul, *Farewell But Not Goodbye*, Hodder and Stoughton, 2005
Spencer, Adam, *Wembley and Kingsbury*, Alan Sutton Publishing, 1995
Taw, Thomas, *Football's War and Peace; The Tumultuous Season of 1946-47*, Desert Island Books, 2003
Vigon, Tim, *One Hundred Greatest Footballers*, Generation Publications, 1999

Articles, Journals, Magazines, Newspapers, Programmes
Book of Football, Marshall Cavendish, 1972
'Empire What Empire? Imperialism and British National Identity, circa 1815-1914', Prof. Bernard Potter, Emeritus Professor of History at the University of Newcastle
50th Wembley F.A.Cup Final programme, Arsenal v Ipswich, 6/5/78
The Guardian, 6/5/06, 3/6/06
London Evening Standard, 20/2/06
Manchester Evening News, 13/6/06
Metro News 14/6/06
Shoot!; 27th November 1971, 22nd January 1972, 8th April 1972, 9th March 1973, 15th January 1977, 26th March 1977, 24th December 1977, 25th February 1978, 15th April 1978
'St. George and the Dragon', Don Aldridge, England v Wales programme, 20/5/81
'Schoolboy Soccer Rarely fails to please', Jack Rollin, England v France Schoolboy International programme, 5th June 1976
Sportspages Lecture 1999, 'A Wild Orgy Of Speed: Responses To Speedway In Britain Before The Second World War', Jack Williams
Stockcar Magazine, September and October 1974
'Technical skill, attacking style, fierce passion, that's Argentina', Jack

Rollin, England v Argentina programme 22/5/74
Widnes R.L.F.C. Hall of Fame Brochure, Sam Patmore, Ron Girvin, Stephen Fox, John Potter & Chris Moore

Websites
Abbey Pynford: www.abbeypynford.co.uk
Arikah travel guide portal: www.arikah.com
Arundel & Brighton Walking Pilgrimages: www.thepilgrims.org.uk
Ballparks by Munsey & Suppes: www.ballparks.com/
Boxing Memorabilia: www.boxing-memorabilia.com
BBC Sport: www.bbc.co.uk
Bradford Bulls: www.bradfordbulls.co.uk
Brent Heritage: www.brent-heritage.co.uk
British Greyhounds Racing Board: www.thedogs.co.uk
Eastside Boxing: www.eastsideboxing.com
The English Football Archive: www.the-english-football-archive.com
England Football on-line: www.englandfootballonline.com
England Hockey: www.englandhockey.co.uk
Era of the Biff (Rugby League) Jeff Quigley, www.eraofthebiff.com
Everton F.C.: www.evertonfc.com
Exeter Speedway The County Ground Years : www.exeter-falcons.demon.co.uk/index.html
FC Barcelona: www.fcbarcelona.com
Football Association: www.thefa.com
Football Focus: www. footballfocus.xsmnet.com
ESPN Soccernet : www.soccernet.com
Guardian Unlimited : www.guardian.co.uk
HOK Sport : www.hoksve.com
Institute for War & Peace Reporting, Baku Celebrates its Wembley Hero: www.iwpr.net
Liverpool F.C.: www.liverpoolfc.tv
London Borough of Brent: www.brent.gov.uk
Lyrics Freak: www.lyricsfreak.com
Motorcycle Museum Hall of Fame : www.motorcyclemuseum.org/halloffame/
National Football Museum : www.nationalfootballmuseum.com/
Oxford United: www.thisisunited.com
Planet World Cup: www.planetworldcup.com
Popsmear: www.popsmear.com/popculture/features/17/evel.html
Queen Online: www.queenonline.com
Railway Archive: www.railwayarchive.org.uk
Rolling Start – Dave Carter: www.rollingstart.co.uk
Rolling Stones Complete Recording Sessions: www.stonessessions.com
Rotten Dot Com, Evel Knievel: www.rotten.com/library/bio/entertainers/daredevils/evel-knievel/
Rugby League Programmes and Challenge Cup, Graham Underwood: www.rlprogs.co.uk
Rugby League Hall of Fame : www.rlhalloffame.org.uk
Rugby League History, Sean Fagin: www.RL1908.com
Schooldays : www.lewys.co.uk
Science and Society: www.scienceandsociety.co.uk
St. Helens: www.saints.org.uk
St. Petersburg Times: www.sptimes.ru
Sixties City: www.sixtiescity.com
Sport England: www.sportengland.org/
Sporting Heroes: www.sporting-heroes.net
Steve Magro's History of Speedway: homepages.ihug.com.au/~stv-magro/pages/photogallery.htm
Teenage Wildlife: www.teenagewildlife.com
The Unofficial Live Aid Site: iveaid.free.fr/
Vintage Speedway Magazine: www.motorcycle-uk.com
Watkins Familly History Society: www.watkins.net.au
Wembley National Stadium Limited: www.wembleystadium.com/
Wembley London Ltd: www.whatsonwembley.com/
Wikipedia: www.wikipedia.org

Acknowledgements

The authors would like to thank the following for advice, support, encouragement, quotes and proof-reading: Joy Anning, Charles Brooking, Bridget Halpin, Bert Harkins, Kerry Hegarty, Wendy Rosier Johnson, Michael Kerchey, Keith Knight, Chris Lewington, Nick Packter, Joe Power, Tom Read, Renata Riveiro-Recarey, Ian Roberts, Mark Savage, Holly Sutton-Brand, Timmy Sutton-Brand, Susie Sutton-Pratt, Brigitte Tomsett, Jeff Weston.

Special thanks to Wembley National Stadium Ltd for advice and information.

PHOTOGRAPH/PICTURE CREDITS

Special thanks to:
Tina Morton and colleagues at London Borough of Brent Archive for numerous photos and images
Scottish Football Museum for photos of England v Scotland 1949
Egmont UK Ltd for permission to use the cover of 'Scorcher & Score' 17-7-71
Seguí /FC Barcelona for photos of the 1992 European Cup Final

The Football Association for permission to use World Cup Willie
Leeds Rhinos RFC for photos from the 1999 Rugby League Challenge Cup Final
London Transport Museum for permission to use LTM 365 'Cup Final' 1934 Panel Poster
Dave Carter for stock car racing photos
Andy Davidson for the Wembley 1980s photos (American Football goalposts, Wembley Turf, Player changing rooms/bath, speedway montage)
Wealdstone FC for photo of 1985 FA Trophy Cup Final
Paul Fitzgerald for the drawing of Sir Edward Watkin
Joe Power for photo of the stage of Spice Girls concert
Arundel & Brighton Walking Pilgrimages for photo of Pope John Paul II visit to Wembley 1982
Alejandro Colombo, Argentina for photo of Maracana Stadium
Bert Harkins for photos of Wembley Lions speedway
Chris Brand for photo of Lego Wembley

All other photos by Pete Tomsett